How Many of These Questions Can You Answer?

The answers are inside this gem of a book, along with 1,500 more Fabulous Facts and mountains of Learned Research.

1. How many members of *Our Gang* can you name?

2. Who conducted the Longines Symphonette? Who was the announcer?

3. Who ran for Vice President on the Landon ticket in '36?

4. Who wrote *Abie's Irish Rose*?

5. What magazine timed every feature for its reading speed?

6. Whose theme song was "Deep Forest"?

7. Claire Trevor won her Oscar for what movie?

8. What were tanna leaves?

9. Where did you se

10. Who was the Bare

Other SIGNET Titles You Will Enjoy

The Nostalgia Quiz Book

by Martin A. Gross

A SIGNET BOOK from

NEW AMERICAN LIBRARY

TIMES MIRROR

Published by arrangement with Arlington House, Inc.

THIRD PRINTING

SIGNET, SIGNET CLASSICS, SIGNETTE, MENTOR AND PLUME BOOKS
are published by The New American Library, Inc.,
1301 Avenue of the Americas, New York, New York 10019

FIRST PRINTING, NOVEMBER, 1971

PRINTED IN THE UNITED STATES OF AMERICA

TO MY FATHER AND MOTHER,

WHO REMEMBER

CONTENTS

(Numbers refer to quizzes, not pages)

INTRODUCTION

How much do you remember about yesterday? Can you recall the names of the actors who starred in your favorite movie? Do you remember early television? The hit songs you danced to at your prom? The radio mysteries you listened to under the pillow? The glorious comic strips? The wonderful swing bands? The names, places and happenings that made headlines while you were growing up?

In *The Nostalgia Quiz Book* you'll find over 1,555 questions sorted into 150 quizzes about things you, your friends, and your family most likely enjoyed, read, saw, heard, worried about, and laughed at in the period from about 1919 to 1950.

Why was this particular 31-year slice of memory chosen? It was purely an arbitrary decision. After all, one man's nostalgia is another man's history.

Refusing to trust to his memory, even though it's photographic, or his knowledge of the past, even though it approaches perfection, the apprehensive author checked every answer with either primary sources ("Vas you dere, Sharlie?") or acknowledged authorities. However, the author must grudgingly assume responsibility for any mistakes.

HOW TO USE THIS BOOK

You'll find the 150 quizzes in the front of the book. Each quiz has been given a number. You'll find the answers under the corresponding numbers in the Answer Section beginning on page 257. To find the answers to any quiz, simply look up the same quiz number at the back of the book.

To make things more interesting, each quiz has been categorized, sometimes willy-nilly. (When it comes to classifying things nostalgically, there's bound to be a blurring of the lines. Do you classify a movie musical quiz under movies, music, or singers?)

FOUR WAYS TO HAVE
SOME OLD-FASHIONED FUN WITH THIS BOOK

1. *Time Machine*. Just skip from page to page, testing your memory of things past. From a quiz about Hitchcock films, flip over to a set of questions on batting averages. If still amazed at your knowledge, try your hand at an old radio show quiz. Time-killing idea: take the book along on a trip; you'll be surprised how the hours fly when you're recalling the past.

2. *Categories*. The Table of Contents breaks down all quizzes by subjects. If you're a movie buff, test your expertise on the 35 quizzes about movies. And if "Take the A Train" is your idea of heaven, see how many of the 140 questions about jazz and swing you can answer.

3. *Nostalgia Quiz Party*. Here's an idea for your next party. Choose any category: the movies, hit musicals, famous singers, sports, inventions, etc. Divide the group into two teams. You act as quizmaster. Give each team a question from the same quiz. Record the time it takes the team to answer, but give them a deadline of, say, six minutes. If they strike out, throw the same question at the other team as a bonus. If they can answer the question within the time limit, deduct three minutes from *their* score. No penalty if they miss. Add up the total length of time for each team. The team with the shortest time is the winner.

4. *Fact Collecting*. Browse through The Nostalgia Quiz Book to build up your stock of unimportant, useless but enjoyable general information. You can floor your friends with your tidbits of nostalgia, impress your boss with your knowledge of things gone by, even win local though fleeting fame as an expert on yesteryear. It's more fun than watching a rerun of "Make Room for Daddy."

No matter how you see The Nostalgia Quiz Book, you're sure to have fun. You'll find yourself dredging up things ᵐ your memory bank you thought you'd completely forgotten, indulging in pleasant total recall, and going back to a time when everything seemed simpler and sweeter.

Most importantly, you'll find yourself answering that always intriguing nostalgic question: "Do you remember when you were young?"

1. Immediate Seating in the Balcony

Identify the movie:

1. A phony diplomat is killed with a camera-gun; a windmill sends giant semaphore signals to airplanes; Edmund Gwenn tries to push Joel McCrea off Westminster Cathedral.

_____

2. NAZI: "Heil Hitler."
FRED MACMURRAY: "Nuts to you, dope."
NAZI: "I give you our German greeting, American."
FRED MACMURRAY: "And I gave you ours, dope."
NAZI: "Was heisst das *dope*?"

_____

3. Katherine Hepburn poisons a banquet hall full of Japanese officers.

_____

4. "This is the story of an unconquerable fortress, the American home, 1943 . . ."

_____

5. "I'm only a poor corrupt official." . . . "You despise me, Rick, don't you?" . . . "If I gave you any thought I probably would." . . . "Was that cannon fire—or is it my heart pounding?"

6. Twenty thousand pounds sterling . . . Iago, a pet monkey . . . an emerald necklace . . . a private asylum . . . a dagger in Count Fosco's back.

---

7. A sled named Rosebud . . . "Today—as it must to all men—death came to . . ."

---

8. A big game hunter stalks Hitler.

---

9. An egomaniac breaks his hip and is confined to an average midwestern home, which he turns upside down.

---

10. The victim's head is kept in a hatbox.

2. Comic Queries

1. Superman was faster than a speeding bullet, but what extraterrestrial substance had the power to slow him down?

2. A Power Ring and a Green Lamp gave Green Lantern his awesome power. What took them away?

3. What was the unbelievable name given the foundling in Gasoline Alley?

4. Where would you find Brick Bradford?

5. What was the name of the elves drawn by Palmer Cox?

6. Who drew the famous "Injun Summer" cartoon for *The Chicago Tribune*?

7. Who was Krazy Kat's teammate?

8. What was Smokey Stover's job? (No, he wasn't a notary sojac.)

9. How could you always identify Plastic Man, no matter what shape he was in?

10. Who made up the Young Allies?

3. Remember Them?

𝒟 𝒟 𝒟 𝒟 𝒟 𝒟

1. The author of *The Last Puritan* was a Harvard professor who, the story goes, looked out his window one beautiful April morning and told his class, "Gentlemen, I have a date with spring," walked out and never returned, retiring to Italy. Who was this professional dropout?

_____

2. *Dere Mabel* was the comic classic of World War I. What was its World War II equivalent?

_____

3. A man who helped libraries and a man who helped people help themselves had the same last name. Who were they?

_____

4. Jeanette MacDonald and Lillian Roth starred in *The Love Parade*. Who played Count Alfred Renard?

_____

5. Rex Harrison was Professor Higgins in *My Fair Lady*. Who was the professor in the 1938 movie, *Pygmalion*?

_____

6. Who played Oliver to Dorothy McGuire's Laura in *The Enchanted Cottage*?

_____

7. What was the name of archy's feline friend?

_____

8. Who were "the seven blocks of granite"?

9. What was the name of George and Marion Kirby's disappearing dog in *Topper*?

10. One of the world's greatest bassos, this opera star began two new careers in middle age: he was the male lead in a triumphant Broadway musical, and he had his own TV show. Who was he?

4. Jukebox Jamboree

Match the song with the artist most associated with it:

1.	Ames Brothers	a)	"My Foolish Heart"
2.	Andrews Sisters	b)	"See What The Boys in The Backroom Will Have"
3.	Eddy Arnold	c)	"Tico-Tico"
4.	Gene Austin	d)	"Wake The Town and Tell The People"
5.	Kenny Baker	e)	"Oh, Johnny, Oh, Johnny, Oh"
6.	Wee Bonnie Baker	f)	"My Blue Heaven"
7.	Cab Calloway	g)	"Bei Mir Bist du Schön"
8.	Mindy Carson	h)	"Naughty Lady of Shady Lane"
9.	Rosemary Clooney	i)	"Bouquet of Roses"
10.	Ethel Smith	j)	"Love Walked In"
11.	Emery Deutsch	k)	"Minnie the Moocher"
12.	Marlene Dietrich	l)	"Botch-a-Me"
13.	Morton Downey	m)	"Play, Fiddle, Play"
14.	Jimmy Durante	n)	"Carolina Moon"
15.	Billy Eckstein	o)	"Umbriago"

5. Buying Spree

1. Who sponsored "The First Nighter"?

_____

2. What product was advertised through open letters written by Jim Henry (Salesman)?

_____

3. What product used the slogan "Ten Shots Quick"?

_____

4. What two pipe tobaccos had the same names as articles of men's formal wear?

_____

5. Complete the name of this product: "Hind's Honey—."

_____

6. Which word does not belong: Kolynos, Colgate's, Sloan's, Iodent?

_____

7. What famous first was the Queensboro Realty Corp. responsible for: a) first radio sponsor, 1922; b) first realty company to sell land in Queens, New York City; c) developer of the first housing project; d) first mail order Florida land developer?

_____

8. Who sponsored "The World of Tomorrow" at the 1939 New York World's Fair?

9. Elsie and Elmer worked for what company?

10. "Gee, dad, it's a ———!"

6. No Business Like Show Biz

1. What actress played in *Rain* for two years?

2. What play had the beat of a tom-tom running through it?

3. Oskar Straus wrote the music for *The Chocolate Soldier*. Who wrote the play on which it was based? And what was the name of the original play?

4. George Gershwin wrote the music for *For Goodness Sake, Lady, Be Good!* and *Funny Face*. Who starred in all three musicals?

5. What was *Lightnin'* famous for?

6. The Federal Theatre Project modernized a Gilbert and Sullivan operetta twice. What were the names of the two new Savoyard productions?

7. This revue opened in 1929. On stage were Fred Allen, Clifton Webb, and Libby Holman. What was its name?

8. Mrs. Hoover strips the White House of spoons, portraits, and the radio aerial. John D. Rockefeller staggers after his son with a knife when he learns the family owns Radio City. In what revue by Moss Hart and Irving Berlin did these curious incidents occur?

9. Who wrote *Abie's Irish Rose*?

10. Mayor Jimmy Walker united Miss Borach and Mr. Rosenberg in wedlock in 1929. What were the more famous names of the bride and groom?

7. People from the Past

1. What did all these men have in common: The Old Man in The Corner, Philip Trent, Lord Peter Wimsey, Max Carrados, and John Thorndyke, K.C.?

_____

2. Who were the Joads?

_____

3. Who were N. C. Wyeth, Maxfield Parrish, and Howard Pyle?

_____

4. What American humorists immortalized: a) the goober; b) the cockroach; c) the bromide?

_____

5. What American poet-biographer was also a folk singer?

_____

6. For what were these men noted: a) Albert Payson Terhune; b) Edward Payson Weston?

_____

7. Can you name the three sisters who gained fame as: a) a poet; b) a novelist; c) an actress?

_____

8. Who was the American novelist whose brother was an eminently successful song writer?

9. What did all these people have in common: Captain Molyneux, Dorian, Adrian, and Chanel?

10. Who wrote *You Can't Go Home Again, Look Homeward, Angel,* and *The Web and The Rock*?

8. Oscars for the Best Actors

Can you match the performers and the movies they gave their Oscar-winning performances in?

1. 1933, *The Private Life of Henry VIII.*   a) Gary Cooper

2. 1934, *It Happened One Night.*   b) Paul Lukas

3. 1935, *The Informer.*   c) Ray Milland

4. 1936, *The Story of Louis Pasteur.*   d) Ronald Colman

5. 1937, *Captains Courageous.*   e) Fredric March

6. 1938, *Boys Town.*   f) Bing Crosby

7. 1939, *Goodbye, Mr. Chips.*   g) James Cagney

8. 1940, *The Philadelphia Story.*   h) Charles Laughton

9. 1941, *Sergeant York.*   i) Clark Gable

10. 1942, *Yankee Doodle Dandy.*   j) Robert Donat

11. 1943, *Watch on the Rhine.*   k) James Stewart

12. 1944, *Going My Way.*   l) Spencer Tracy

13. 1945, *The Lost Weekend.*   m) Victor McLaglen

14. 1946, *The Best Years of Our Lives.*   n) Paul Muni

15. 1947, *A Double Life.*   o) Spencer Tracy

9. Theme Songs on the Radio

1. What was the very appropriate theme song of "Mr. Keen, Tracer of Lost Persons"? And who was the composer?

_____

2. Rossini's "William Tell Overture" was just one of the musical motifs heard on "The Lone Ranger." Can you name two others?

_____

3. "Funiculi-Funicula" was the theme song of what long-running soap opera?

_____

4. "Love Nest" introduced what durable comedy show?

_____

5. "Hello nephews, nieces, mine. I'm glad to see you look so fine. How's mama? How's papa? But tell me first, just how you are . . ." told you that you were listening to what children's program?

_____

6. "We two boys without a care, Entertain you folks out there—That's our hap hap-happiness!" was the theme of what pioneer radio program?

_____

7. "Darling Nellie Gray" opened this soap opera; "Polly Wolly Doodle" closed it. What was its name?

8. Who was "that little chatterbox . . . the one with curly auburn locks?"

---

9. What was the name of Jack Benny's theme song?

---

10. A Chinese gong was the appropriate sound opening this show. What was this terrific adventure program?

10. They Don't Write This Way Anymore

🖋 🖋 🖋 🖋 🖋 🖋 🖋

1. What sort of books did Ralph Henry Barbour write?

---

2. What did these men have in common: John Howard Lawson, Frederick Lonsdale, Sidney Howard, Jacinto Benavente?

---

3. Who was the small town editor who wrote "What's the matter with Kansas?"

---

4. What magazine did Oswald Garrison Villard edit?

---

5. What sort of stories did Albert Payson Terhune write?

---

6. Who wrote *Jeeves* and *Leave It to Psmith*?

---

7. *Dragon's Teeth* won this author a Pulitzer Prize. It was one of 10 volumes in a series. Name the author and the series.

---

8. Who wrote *Marty*?

---

9. Who turned down the 1940 Pulitzer Prize for his play, *The Time of Your Life*?

---

10. Who wrote *Mission to Moscow*?

11. Their Biggest Hits

How many of these artists can you match with their best-known hits?

1. Nelson Eddy
2. Alice Faye
3. Georgia Gibbs
4. Arthur Godfrey

5. Carol Haney

6. Phil Harris
7. Dick Haymes
8. Horace Heidt
9. Hildegarde
10. Libby Holman
11. Bob Hope

12. Lena Horne
13. Eddy Howard
14. Walter Huston
15. Ink Spots

a) "September Song"
b) "Stormy Weather"
c) "Moanin' Low"
d) "Deep in The Heart of Texas"
e) "That's What I Like About The South"
f) "Too Fat Polka"
g) "You'll Never Know"
h) "If I Didn't Care"
i) "To Each His Own"
j) "Thanks For The Memory"
k) "Darling, Je Vous Aime Beaucoup"
l) "Little White Lies"
m) "Steam Heat"
n) "Kiss of Fire"
o) "Short'nin' Bread"

12. Exercise Your Memory Muscles

1. By what name was Florence Nightingale Graham better known?

_____

2. What made Popeye strong?

_____

3. What was the theme song of the 1936 Democratic Presidential campaign?

_____

4. What prison was headed by Lewis E. Lawes?

_____

5. What was Eleanor Roosevelt's maiden name?

_____

6. Who was Dr. Carl Austin Weiss, Jr.?

_____

7. What coin was designed by a man whose initials were V. D. B.?

_____

8. Who sponsored Dr. Cadman's Sunday afternoon inspirational radio talks?

9. What were the Cheka and the OGPU?

10. Who was Chester Gump's uncle?

13. Hollywood Couples

Can you match the famous husband and wife?

1. John Agar	a)	Mary Pickford
2. Bing Crosby	b)	Edna Best
3. Dick Powell	c)	Annabella
4. Tyrone Power	d)	Shirley Temple
5. John Barrymore	e)	Elsa Lancaster
6. Roy Rogers	f)	June Allyson
7. Jacques Bergerac	g)	Dixie Lee
8. Herbert Marshall	h)	Dale Evans
9. Charles Laughton	i)	Ginger Rogers
10. Douglas Fairbanks	j)	Dolores Costello

14. Comic Creators

Try to match the comic strips with the artists who created them:

1. "The Little King"
2. "Polly and Her Pals"
3. "Winnie Winkle"
4. "Gasoline Alley"
5. "Moon Mullins"

6. "Metropolitan Movies"
7. "Mandrake the Magician"
8. "Bringing Up Father"
9. "Little Lulu"
10. "Harold Teen"
11. "Barnaby"
12. "Our Boarding House"
13. "Superman"

14. "Abie the Agent"
15. "Nize Baby"

a) Crockett Johnson
b) Carl Ed
c) Marge
d) William Freyse
e) Jerry Siegel and Joe Shuster
f) Harry Hershfield
g) O. Soglow
h) Milt Gross
i) Cliff Sterrett
j) Martin Branner
k) George McManus
l) Frank King
m) Lee Falk and Phil Davis
n) Frank Willard
o) Denys Wortman

15. Second-Class Reading Matter

Remember magazines? You could get them in black-and-white and/or color. And if you didn't like the commercial, you could just flip the page. You had your choice of humor, double-dome, sports, enjoyable fiction—even news. And whatever happened to cartoons?

1. This magazine timed every feature for its reading speed. What was its name?

_____

2. What magazine featured the *High Hat* and *High Heels* columns?

_____

3. The caviar sophisticates of 1925 ate this magazine up; it wasn't for "the old lady from Dubuque." It's name . . . and first editor?

_____

4. What magazine, founded in 1890, gave up the ghost in the 30s because of a fouled-up opinion poll?

_____

5. Who published *Physical Culture*?

_____

6. What weekly was printed on pink paper?

7. Can you name the magazine that had the same title as a Thackeray novel?

---

8. What magazine was edited by George Jean Nathan and Henry Louis Mencken and published by William Randolph Hearst?

---

9. Britton Hadden helped found what magazine?

---

10. What magazine offered safe anchorage to such salty types as Crunch and Des and Tugboat Annie?

16. Going Places

1. What was the 1923 MacFarland noted for?

---

2. What was the cheapest Ford ever built? Can you guess its approximate price?

3. What was the USS *Langley*'s claim to fame?

_____

4. What was the difference between a railway company and a railroad company?

_____

5. What was the name of the airplane in which Wiley Post soloed around the world?

_____

6. What was the distinguishing feature of the Knight type motor?

_____

7. Who was the U. S. naval officer who photographed the North Pole in 1926?

_____

8. What was the transmission system used in Ford autos in the 20s?

_____

9. Under what river is the Holland Tunnel?

_____

10. Where did Dr. Grenfell carry on his missionary work?

17. Sporting Types

1. Who was Major H. O. D. Segrave?

_____

2. What breed of dog was Laddie Boy and to whom did he belong?

_____

3. Who succeeded Jack Johnson as heavyweight champ?

_____

4. With what sport were the following men identified: Donoghue, Butwell, Parke, Robinson, Sande?

_____

5. With what sport were these men identified: Ketchel, Sharkey, Nelson, La Motta, Mauriello?

_____

6. Arne Borg was prominent in what sport?

_____

7. Sabin Carr of Yale distinguished himself in what sport?

_____

8. In what sport was Ralph Greenleaf a world champion?

9. What did these men have in common: Alf Shrubb, Tom Longboat, Hannes Kolehmainen, and Jean Bouin?

10. In what sport were Lewis, Stecher, and Munn names to contend with?

18. Who's Really Who?

Match the person with his or her occupation:

1.	Wilbur L. Cross	a)	balloonist
2.	Charles Hurley	b)	billiards player
3.	Harold L. Ickes	c)	actor
4.	Benjamin Cardozo	d)	Secretary of Labor
5.	Margaret Fishback	e)	Mayor of New York City
6.	Burgess Meredith	f)	Governor of Connecticut
7.	Frances Perkins	g)	Secretary of the Interior
8.	Willie Hoppe	h)	Governor of Massachusetts
9.	Auguste Piccard	i)	writer
10.	William O'Dwyer	j)	Supreme Court Justice

34

19. A Matter of Business

1. What did the initials T B I just above the lens on a Kodak Brownie stand for?

_____

2. What auto had a concave hexagon in its hubcap?

_____

3. What firm was advertised by the Happiness Boys?

_____

4. What product was advertised by a band of singers who opened their show with "Smiles"?

_____

5. What were the call letters of Westinghouse Electric's pioneer radio station?

_____

6. The advertising of what product made "halitosis" a household word?

_____

7. What college changed its name to benefit from the bequest of a tobacco manufacturer?

_____

8. What did the D. in John Rockefeller stand for?

9. Who was the candy bar "Baby Ruth" named after?

10. Who bought the first Hammond Electric Organ: a) Jose Iturbi, in 1940; b) George Gershwin, in 1935; c) Ignace Paderewski, in 1922; d) Harry S. Truman, in 1947?

20. Oscars for the Best Actresses

Can you match the actresses and the movies they gave their Oscar-winning performances in?

1. 1933, *Morning Glory*	a)	Vivien Leigh
2. 1934, *It Happened One Night*	b)	Ginger Rogers
3. 1935, *Dangerous*	c)	Joan Fontaine
4. 1936, *The Great Ziegfeld*	d)	Ingrid Bergman
5. 1937, *The Good Earth*	e)	Claudette Colbert
6. 1938, *Jezebel*	f)	Katherine Hepburn
7. 1939, *Gone With The Wind*	g)	Loretta Young
8. 1940, *Kitty Foyle*	h)	Bette Davis
9. 1941, *Suspicion*	i)	Greer Garson
10. 1942, *Mrs. Miniver*	j)	Luise Rainer
11. 1943, *The Song of Bernadette*	k)	Joan Crawford
12. 1944, *Gaslight*	l)	Jennifer Jones
13. 1945, *Mildred Pierce*	m)	Luise Rainer
14. 1946, *To Each His Own*	n)	Olivia de Havilland
15. 1947, *The Farmer's Daughter*	o)	Bette Davis

21. Adventurous Blanks

Fill in the missing lines:

1. "And it shall be my duty as District Attorney, not only
[a] _____]
all persons accused of crimes [b] _____], but to
defend with equal vigor [c] _____]."

---

2. "A fiery horse with the speed of light, [a] _____]
The Lone Ranger! With his faithful Indian companion,
Tonto, the [b] _____] masked rider of the plains
led the [c] _____] in the early Western United
States. Nowhere in the pages of history can one [d] _____
_____]. Return with us now to [e] _____]. . .
from out of the past come the [f] _____]. The Lone
Ranger rides again!"

---

3. "Wave the flag for Hudson High, boys,
   [a] _____]
Ever shall our team be champion
Known throughout the land!
Rah Rah Boola Boola Boola Boola
Boola Boola Boola Boo Rah Rah Rah.
   [b] _____]
They're whole wheat with all of the bran.
   [c] _____]
For wheat is the best food of man!
They're crispy and crunchy the whole year through.
Jack Armstrong never tires of them
   [d] _____]
   [e] _____]
The best breakfast food in the land!"

4. "I am the Whistler. And I know [a) _____].
I know many strange tales [b) _____].
Yes. . . . I know the [c) _____] of which they
dare not speak."

22. By Their Themes You Shall Know Them

How many orchestra leaders can you match with their theme songs?

1.	"Take the A Train"	a)	Earl Hines
2.	"Cherokee"	b)	Guy Lombardo
3.	"One O'Clock Jump"	c)	Duke Ellington
4.	"Thinking of You"	d)	Gray Gordon
5.	"Deep Forest"	e)	Count Basie
6.	"I'm Gettin' Sentimental Over You"	f)	Glen Gray
7.	"Time On My Hands"	g)	Kay Kyser
8.	"Nightmare"	h)	Charlie Barnet
9.	"Smoke Rings"	i)	Tommy Dorsey
10.	"Auld Lang Syne"	j)	Artie Shaw

23. Marxmanship

Match the Marx Brothers movie with the character played by Groucho:

1. Mr. Hammer
2. Captain Jeffrey T. Spaulding
3. Professor Quincey Adams Wagstaff
4. Rufus T. Firefly
5. Otis B. Driftwood
6. Dr. Hugo Z. Hackenbush
7. Gordon Miller
8. J. Cheever Loophole
9. S. Quentin Quale
10. Wolf J. Flywheel
11. Ronald Kornblow
12. Sam Grunion

a) *Love Happy*
b) *A Night in Casablanca*
c) *The Cocoanuts*
d) *Go West*
e) *At The Circus*
f) *The Big Store*
g) *Room Service*
h) *A Day at The Races*
i) *Duck Soup*
j) *A Night at The Opera*
k) *Horse Feathers*
l) *Animal Crackers*

24. Preterit Tense

1. Who was the war correspondent who wrote *Brave Men* and *Here is Your War*?

2. What was the name of: a) the ocean liner that burned eight miles off the New Jersey coast in 1934; b) the liner that burned while moored in New York Harbor?

3. Who was "The Sentimental Gentleman of Swing"?

4. Who wrote *The Silver Chalice, Below the Salt, The Tontine,* and *High Towers*?

5. Who wrote these inspirational books: a) *Life Begins at Forty*; b) *Peace of Mind*; c) *Peace of Soul*?

6. Rockefeller Range is in Little America. Where is Little America?

7. Where were the following grand hotels: a) Adlon; b) Astor; c) Shepheards; d) Grand Union?

8. Dr. Barnes founded one of the largest, if least veiwed, art collections in the world. What was his other claim to fame?

9. Who were these people: The Rev. George Fox, The Rev. Clark Poling, Father John Washington, and Rabbi Alexander Goode?

10. Captain Andy Hawks skippered what kind of boat? What was her name?

25. Late Show Memories

1. What was Appolonia Chalupek's movie name?

_____

2. What was the name of the 1940 movie made from Thornton Wilder's play, starring William Holden and Martha Scott?

_____

3. Irene Dunne played Sabra Cravat; Richard Dix was Yancey Cravat; the story was by Edna Ferber. The movie?

_____

4. Who were the juvenile stars of: a) *One Hundred Men and a Girl*; b) *Captains Courageous*; c) *The Kid*; a) *National Velvet*; e) *The Little Colonel*?

_____

5. In what movie were Cathie and Heathcliff the leading characters?

_____

6. Later to become a popular novelist, this screen star's early writings also aroused interest. At her 1935 divorce trial, her diaries created headlines, because they contained "the names of Hollywood's best Romeos." Name the star.

_____

7. Who played: a) Young Dr. Kildare (in the movies); b) Dr. Christian; c) Dr. Gillespie?

8. Claire Trevor won her Oscar for what movie?

9. What was the name of the first Hope, Lamour, Crosby "Road" picture?

10. Who was Marlene Dietrich's leading man in her first American movie (1930)? And what was the name of the movie?

26. Past Perfect Quotes

Who said:

1. "Nobody shoots at Santa Claus."

2. "oh i should worry and fret
    death and i will coquette
    there s a dance in the old dame yet
    toujours gai toujours gai"

_____

3. "The fog comes on little cat feet."

_____

4. "That's all there is: there isn't any more."

_____

5. "Who put pineapple juice in my pineapple juice?"

_____

6. "I never met a man I didn't like."

_____

7. "I shall return."

_____

8. "When the One Great Scorer
     Comes to write against your name—
     He marks—not that you won or
        lost—but how you played the game."

_____

9. "It takes a heap o'livin' in a house
     t' make it home."

_____

10. "A big butter-and-egg man."

27. Hitchcock's Clues

Match the item with the Hitchcock film it was a vital part of:

1. A monogrammed pillowcase
2. The corpse
3. Reverse-sailing windmills
4. An incriminating ring
5. A crop duster
6. A concealed compass
7. A motel shower
8. A wine cellar key
9. An hypnotic portrait
10. A shrunken head

a) *The Paradine Case*
b) *Psycho*
c) *Shadow of a Doubt*
d) *The Trouble With Harry*
e) *Under Capricorn*
f) *Notorious*
g) *Lifeboat*
h) *Rebecca*
i) *Foreign Correspondent*
j) *North by Northwest*

28. Comic Book Rogues' Gallery

Try to pair the villains and the good guys they had it in for:

BAD	GOOD
1. Mr. Freeze	**a)** Flash Gordon
2. Captain Nazi	**b)** Crimebuster
3. The Red Skull	**c)** Batman
4. Black Pete	**d)** The Lone Ranger
5. Bluto	**e)** Captain America
6. The Dragon Lady	**f)** Mickey Mouse
7. Pruneface	**g)** Popeye
8. Ironjaw	**h)** Terry
9. Emperor Ming of Mongo	**i)** Dick Tracy
10. Butch Cavendish	**j)** Captain Marvel

29. Airwave Match

How many radio programs can you identify by their catch-phrases?

1. "Oh, is that you, Myrt?" . . . "Dad-rat the dad-ratted . . ." "How do you you do, I'm sure . . ." "Heavenly days . . ." "Why mister, why mister, why mister, why?"

a) "The Breakfast Club"

2. "Uh-uh-uh . . . don't touch that dial! It's time for . . ."

b) "Beulah"

3. "Each in his own words, Each in his own way. For a world united in peace, Bow your heads and let us pray."

c) "I Love a Mystery"

4. "Send in two inches of the strip of tin that comes off a can of Cocomalt when you open it."

d) "Fibber McGee and Molly"

5. "On the con-positively-trary!"

e) "Blondie"

6. "I'm only thwee and a half years old. I'm a b-a-a-d boy."

f) "The Jack Benny Program"

7. "Honest to my grandma."

g) "Buck Rogers in the 25th Century"

8. "I'm feeling mighty low."

h) "Abbott and Costello Program"

9. "No names, please!"

i) "The Jimmy Durante Show"

10. "Anaheim, Azusa, and Cuc-a-monga."

j) "The Goodwill Hour"

30. Strange Things Are Happening

1. What was the name of the henchman of: a) Count Dracula; b) Prof. Moriarty?

2. What were tanna leaves?

3. Who played the Angel Athanael in *The Horn Blows at Midnight*?

4. Who was the movie star who had a 36-foot chest span. (Hint: his ears were one foot long.)

5. Mytel, Tytel, Tylo, and Tylette were a few of the characters who went into the Lands of Memory and Luxury in this Technicolor extravaganza. Can you name it?

---

6. What do all these actors have in common: Emil Jannings, Adolphe Menjou, Walter Huston, Ray Milland, Ray Walston, Laird Cregar, and Claude Rains?

---

7. What do all these actors have in common: Sheldon Lewis, John Barrymore, Conrad Veidt, Fredric March, and Spencer Tracy?

---

8. Who whistled "In the Hall of The Mountain King" whenever murder was on his mind?

---

9. There were two doctors in *The Hound of the Baskervilles* (1935). Dr. Watson was played by Nigel Bruce. Who played Dr. Mortimer?

---

10. In *The Island of Lost Souls*, Dr. Moreau enslaved an ape man, The Sayer of the Law. Who played Moreau, and who was The Sayer of the Law?

31. Limelight

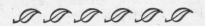

1. Lou Clayton was one of a famous trio in *Show Girl*. Name the other two members of the group.

_____

2. What famous comic twirled a lariat during his act? What comic used a pool cue as a prop? What comic juggled?

_____

3. Who was the Scottish entertainer knighted for his services during World War I?

_____

4. Name the shows that closed with these lines: a) "Hey, Flagg, wait for baby!"; b) "I'm going to be baptized, damn it!"; c) "How they are cheering, Albert. If only you could have been here."; d) "God damn dear old . . . No, God bless dear old Charlie . . . who passed beyond desire, has all the luck at last."

_____

5. Who was Joe Jackson?

_____

6. What did these have in common: Pantages, Orpheum, Poli, Loew, Proctor?

_____

7. Who was the dancer who joined the Royal Flying Corps in World War I and crashed to his death in Texas?

8. Who asked people, "Wanna buy a duck?"

9. Who did a vaudeville monolog explaining why he couldn't imitate four Hawaiians?

10. Who was Billie Burke's husband?

32. Showing Your Age

1. Can you give the first names of these famous people: a) Sister Kenny; b) Mahatma Gandhi; c) Premier Lenin; d) Il Duce?

2. What was the name of the hog that won the first prize in *State Fair*?

3. Who was the politician associated with the song, "The Sidewalks of New York"?

_____

4. What was meant by the phrase, "Tinker to Evers to Chance"?

_____

5. What comic strip was created by Arthur R. Momand?

_____

6. Who invented the Orgone Box?

_____

7. Where did you send the Ralston box tops?

_____

8. What was the name of Tom Mix's ranch?

_____

9. Who popularized the statement: "Every day in every way, I'm getting better and better"?

_____

10. Who was the barefoot boy from Wall Street?

33. Who Played Whom?

𝒟 𝒟 𝒟 𝒟 𝒟 𝒟

Name the star who played the star:

THE ONE AND ONLY	THE IMPERSONATOR
1. Nellie Melba	a) Ann Blyth
2. George M. Cohan	b) Errol Flynn
3. Edwin Booth	c) James Cagney
4. Joe E. Lewis	d) Susan Hayward
5. John Barrymore	e) Patrice Munsel
6. Nora Bayes	f) Betty Hutton
7. Eva Tanguay	g) Richard Burton
8. Texas Guinan	h) Mitzi Gaynor
9. Helen Morgan	i) Ann Sheridan
10. Jane Froman	j) Frank Sinatra

34. Writers and Their Writing

𝒟 𝒟 𝒟 𝒟 𝒟 𝒟

1. Sportswriters frequently became known for their work in other genres. Who were the sports writers who wrote: a) *Money From Home*; b) *You Know Me Al*; c) *Snow Goose*; d) *George Spelvin, American*?

___

2. He thought *Wanderer of the Wasteland* was his most mature and finished work. But out of his more than sixty books, the public liked *Riders of the Purple Sage* best. Who was he?

3. In 1923, the twenty-seventh volume in a seemingly endless saga was published. Like all the others, it starred Dick, Tom, and Sam. What was the name of this series?

4. This Pulitzer Prize author wrote *Early Autumn, The Rains Came, The Strange Case of Miss Annie Spragg,* and *Pleasant Valley.* In 1933 he bought a 600-acre farm near Mansfield, Ohio, and named it Malabar. What was his name?

5. Orson Welles made a movie from this Indiana author's book, *The Magnificent Ambersons,* but he is probably best known for *Penrod* and *Seventeen.* What was his name?

6. Who wrote: a) *Anthony Adverse*; b) *Northwest Passage*; c) *Java Head*; d) *Mutiny on the Bounty*?

7. Who created Jurgen, the paunchy pawnbroker of Poictesme?

8. What was Babbitt's first name?

9. *Kiss The Boys Goodbye* and *The Women* were written by a beautiful woman playwright. Her name?

10. With Charles MacArthur he wrote *The Front Page.* On his own he wrote *Erik Dorn.* Who was he?

35. Some of Alfred's Pictures

❦ ❦ ❦ ❦ ❦ ❦

Match the Hitchcock film with the vital "piece of business":

1. A bloodstained doll
2. A missing finger
3. An incriminating cigaret lighter
4. Crashing cymbals
5. Milk chocolates on an assembly line
6. Latch keys
7. A doctored drink

8. A wedding ring
9. A twitching eye

10. A cat

a) *To Catch A Thief*
b) *Rear Window*
c) *Dial M for Murder*

d) *Stage Fright*
e) *Strangers on a Train*

f) *Secret Agent*
g) *Young and Innocent (The Girl Was Young)*
h) *The Lady Vanishes*
i) *The Man Who Knew Too Much*
j) *The 39 Steps*

36. When Tuesday Night Was Berle Night

❦ ❦ ❦ ❦ ❦ ❦

1. Name the cast of "Mr. Peepers."

_____

2. Who played Clarence Day, Sr., on "Life with Father"?

_____

3. Who was the Indian mentalist who read sealed messages while his eyes were taped shut?

_____

4. What do all these people have in common: pianist Eugene List, Dean Martin and Jerry Lewis, Richard Rodgers and Oscar Hammerstein II, and fight referee Ruby Goldstein?

_____

5. Many years and many pounds after his success as a silent screen boy actor, who starred with Jack Webb on "Dragnet"?

_____

6. Who played Percy Dovetonsils?

_____

7. Who invented droodles?

_____

8. Who was the Kupke Kid?

_____

9. In addition to Sid Caesar, Imogene Coca, Carl Reiner, and Howard Morris, who else was featured on "Your Show of Shows"?

_____

10. William Bendix was the most famous Chester Riley, but who was the first?

37. Real Magic

Complete these childhood incantations:

1. "Step on a crack . . ."

   _____

2. "Takes one . . ."

   _____

3. "Finders keepers . . ."

   _____

4. "I'm rubber . . ."

   _____

5. "Ink a bink . . ."

38. Hollywood at War

Identify the war movie from the names of these players:

1. John Gilbert, Renée Adorée.

2. Clark Gable, Walter Pidgeon, Van Johnson, Brian Donlevy.

3. William Holden, Grace Kelly, Mickey Rooney.

4. Jean Harlow, Ben Lyon, James Hall.

5. Preston Foster, Lloyd Nolan, William Bendix.

6. Ray Milland, William Holden, Veronica Lake.

7. William Holden, Alec Guinness, Jack Hawkins.

8. Burgess Meredith, Robert Mitchum.

9. Van Johnson, John Hodiak, Ricardo Montalban.

10. John Wayne, Kirk Douglas, Patricia Neal.

39. Don't Look Back Now

1. What planet was discovered in 1930?

_____

2. What did all these have in common: *Thrilling Wonder, Astounding, Amazing, Doc Savage, Planet, Galaxy?*

_____

3. Identify: a) The Warbling Banjoist; b) The Redheaded Music Maker; c) The Street Singer; d) The Idol of the Airlines.

_____

4. Who was: a) Mischa, b) Jascha; c) Toscha?

_____

5. Who was Eugene Sandow?

_____

6. Who wore the number "77"?

_____

7. What kind of animal was adopted by Claude Jarman, Jr., in *The Yearling?*

_____

8. Who played Livingstone to Spencer Tracy's Stanley in *Stanley and Livingstone?*

9. Paul Muni played the French writer in *The Life of Emile Zola*. Who played Captain Dreyfus?

10. Who produced "Your Show of Shows"?

40. Strip-Tease

Can you match the dull everyday person with his comic-strip hero alter ego?

1. Clark Kent
2. Steve Rogers
3. Bruce Wayne
4. Billy Batson
5. Freddie Freeman
6. Jim Barr
7. Captain Albright

a) Captain Midnight
b) Superman
c) Bullet Man
d) Captain America
e) Batman
f) Captain Marvel, Jr.
g) Captain Marvel

41. When Test Patterns Were Prime-Time Viewing

1. What was Jimmy Nelson's dummy's name?

_____

2. Who was the star of "Those Two"?

_____

3. Who was the host of "Broadway Open House"?

_____

4. Who told you to "put a little fun in your life—try dancing"?

_____

5. How many of the second bananas can you remember from Steve Allen's first show?

_____

6. Who hosted "You Asked for It"?

_____

7. Who was Julia Meade?

_____

8. Who fired whom for "lack of humility"?

———————

9. What was the name of the super-sophisticated character played by Renzo Cesana?

———————

10. Who said: a) "Tell you what I'm gonna do!"; b) "Well, I'll be a dirty bird!"; and c) "Wait for me, Wild Bill!"?

42. Sports Page

☙ ☙ ☙ ☙ ☙ ☙

1. "Joltin' Joe . . . We want you on our side" was the line of a popular song in the 40s. Who was "Joltin' Joe"?

———————

2. Who was the "Wild Bull of the Pampas"?

———————

3. Who was the "Big Six"?

———————

4. Who was "The Cinderella Man"?

———————

5. In what country was Knute Rockne born? Who played him in the movie?

6. Who was "The Manassa Mauler"?

7. What is known as "The House That Ruth Built"?

8. What athletic coach was nicknamed "Hurry-Up"?

9. What heavyweight credited his defeat of Max Baer to the study of yoga?

10. With what sport were Tommy Milton and Jimmy Murphy associated?

43. Author, Meet the Quizzers

✑ ✑ ✑ ✑ ✑ ✑

1. Name the authors of: a) *The Good Earth*; b) *The Crisis*; c) *The Sun Also Rises*; d) *The Sea Wolf*.

2. *Ferdinand* was the story of a ———; *Bambi* was the story of a ———; *Stuart Little* was the story of a ———; and *Babar* was the story of an ———.

3. Where was each book set: a) *As the Earth Turns*; b) *Shadows on The Rock*; c) *Victory*; d) *Lost Horizon*; e) *Three Cities?*

4. What famous book of the 20s did Dikran Kouyoumdjian write?

5. Who wrote the short stories about Cappy Ricks?

6. Who wrote *Certain People of Importance?*

7. What university president edited a collection of the world's classics?

8. Who wrote the "Tutt" stories about a lawyer?

9. Who turned down the 1926 Pulitzer Prize for the best American novel?

10. What was the "Chesterbelloc"?

44. Calendar Leaves

1. Clifton Fadiman emceed a popular radio quiz show. Oscar Levant livened it up. What was its name?

_____

2. "Brother, Can You Spare A Dime?" was the Depression's song of despair; "Who's Afraid of the Big Bad Wolf?", its song of hope. In what movie was the latter first heard?

_____

3. In August 1948, Mrs. Oksana Kasenkina jumped from a Manhattan building—her object, freedom. From what building did she hurl herself?

_____

4. What did these people have in common: Myra Hess, Jose Iturbi, Josef Hoffman, and Vladimir de Pachmann?

_____

5. Who was The Glacier Priest?

_____

6. Who was the father of tree surgery: a) Luther Burbank; b) John Davey; c) Morris Fishbein; or d) Harvey Cushing?

_____

7. Whose dog, Tige, tagged along after him?

_____

8. What was Coolidge's position before he became vice president?

9. Clarence H. Mackay was an industrialist of the 20s who became the father-in-law of an even more celebrated personality. What company did Mackay head . . . and who was his son-in-law?

---

10. What was a jitney?

45. Gable Television

Match the Gable movie with the description given by your local TV schedule:

    a)   *It Happened One Night*
    b)   *Laughing Sinners*
    c)   *Night Nurse*
    d)   *Susan Lennox*
    e)   *The Secret Six*
    f)   *A Free Soul*
    g)   *The Finger Points*
    h)   *Too Hot to Handle*
    i)   *The Hucksters*
    j)   *Never Let Me Go*

1. Hank and Carl are newspaper reporters investigating gangland killings. With Wallace Beery and Jean Harlow.

2. Louis Blanco is a gangster chief exposed by Breckenridge Lee. With Richard Barthelmess and Fay Wray.

3. Philip Sutherland, a foreign correspondent, and diplomat Christopher St. John Denny are deported from Russia, and forced to leave their wives behind. With Gene Tierney and Theodore Bikel.

4. Incognito heiress Ellie Andrews meets newspaper reporter Peter Warne on a bus and they decide to travel together. With Claudette Colbert.

5. Vic Norman is an ad man who quits Madison Avenue for the good life with society girl Kay Dorrance. With Deborah Kerr, Ava Gardner, and Sidney Greenstreet.

6. Successful engineer Rodney Spencer rescues Helga, a farm girl, from a life of prostitution.

7. Alma Harding asks newsreel cameramen Chris Hunter and Bill Dennis to help find her brother, missing in South America. Hunter films the rescue, becomes famous, wins Alma. With Myrna Loy and Walter Pidgeon.

8. Carl Loomis is a Salvation Army worker who reforms showgirl Ivy Stevens. With Joan Crawford and Neil Hamilton.

9. Gambler Ace Wilfong has an affair with Jan Ashe. He brutalizes her and is murdered by her ex-fiancé, Dwight Winthrop. With Norma Shearer and Leslie Howard.

---

10. Nick, a chauffeur, intends to murder two children and marry their wealthy mother. With Barbara Stanwyck and Joan Blondell.

46. Goin' Steady

Li'l Abner did marry Daisy Mae and Tess Trueheart finally landed Dick Tracy, but most comic-strip heroes and heroines were too busy being heroic to pop the question. Can you name their patient pals?

1. Unable to leap tall buildings in a single bound or even change into something more casual in a telephone booth, poor ——————— couldn't please either Superman or Clark Kent.

---

2. Jim Barr wasn't any high fashion milliner, but his gravity helmet invention was worn with real dash by ———————.

3. Bob accompanied the Queen of the Jungle around the veldt and savannah. Was there ever any real thought of romance in ————'s mind? Nope.

4. Popeye the Sailor's angular girl friend was ————.

5. All-American teenager Archie Andrews had two girls to choose between: the blonde ———— and ————, the brunette.

6. Name the steady boyfriends of Nancy and Little Lulu.

7. Can you name at least four of Steve Canyon's girl friends?

8. Mandrake and Ibis made magic with ———— and ————, respectively.

9. Apparition that he was, the Spirit was still flesh and blood to ————.

10. Longfellow probably turned in his grave when the cartoonist who created Red Man gave this name to our red-faced hero's girl, ————.

47. Ladies of the Pen

Can you identify these famous women writers from these hints?

1. She described her life as "a peculiar treasure."

_____

2. Jalna was the scene of many of this writer's novels.

_____

3. Before hitting the bestselling list, she worked in a hardware store.

_____

4. This author's *Three Weeks* shocked England and the U.S. and introduced "It."

_____

5. She burnt her candle at both ends.

_____

6. She wrote *Five Little Peppers and How They Grew.*

_____

7. In *The Way of the World*, she said, "Laugh and the whole world laughs with you."

_____

8. Bab, a subdeb, and Tish were her heroines.

9. Dr. Lavender, a kindly old clergyman, played an important part in her novels and stories.

---

10. Her sister's name was Eileen.

48. Featured Names

♫ ♫ ♫ ♫ ♫ ♫

1. What was the name of the Duchess of Windsor before she married the Duke?

---

2. Aside from their British nationality, what did Winston Churchill and Charles Chaplin have in common?

---

3. In 1941, this important New Dealer was made executive secretary of the war cabinet. His name?

_____

4. Who was Democratic candidate for vice president in 1920?

_____

5. Who swore in Calvin Coolidge as President?

_____

6. Who was Secretary of Commerce under Coolidge?

_____

7. Father and son served as Secretary of Agriculture. What were their names, and the names of the presidents under whom they served?

_____

8. Who said, "I wanna make the King of England keep his blasted snoot out of America!"?

_____

9. This organization was formed March 15-17, 1919. It was chartered September 16 of the same year by Congress. Can you name it?

_____

10. What was Boyle's Thirty Acres?

49. The Songs That Made Them Famous, or Vice Versa

 🖋 🖋 🖋 🖋 🖋 🖋

Match the artist and the melody associated with him:

1.	Gordon Jenkins	a)	"Don't Fence Me In"
2.	George Jessel	b)	"Blow, Gabriel, Blow"
3.	Allan Jones	c)	"I Wanna Be Loved By You"
4.	Helen Kane	d)	"Puttin' on the Ritz"
5.	Dorothy Lamour	e)	"Manhattan Towers"
6.	Frances Langford	f)	"Thanks a Million"
7.	Ted Lewis	g)	"My Mother's Eyes"
8.	Ella Logan	h)	"Bill"
9.	Groucho Marx	i)	"The Donkey Serenade"
10.	Ethel Merman	j)	"I'm Looking Over a Four Leaf Clover"
11.	Art Mooney	k)	"Moon of Manakoora"
12.	Helen Morgan	l)	"Hurray for Captain Spaulding"
13.	Dick Powell	m)	"I'm in the Mood for Love"
14.	Harry Richman	n)	"How Are Things in Glocca Morra?"
15.	Roy Rogers	o)	"Me and My Shadow"

50. Flying High

1. Glenn L. Martin built this medium bomber for the Army Air Corps. It had a thousand-mile range, carried a payload of three thousand to four thousand pounds of bombs. What was it?

_____

2. Major Thomas Scott Baldwin died at the age of 69 in 1923. What was his contribution to aviation?

_____

3. Who invented the hydroplane?

_____

4. What was the Blenheim?

_____

5. What did Juan de la Cierva invent?

_____

6. How long did it take Howard Hughes and his four companions to fly around the world?

_____

7. Who made the first solo flight around the world?

_____

8. What dirigible made the first commercial transatlantic flight?

9. Who flew from Italy to the Chicago World's Fair with a fleet of twenty-four seaplanes?

10. On October 26, 1929, Mrs. T. W. Evans of Miami, Fla., achieved a flighty sort of fame, because she was: a) the first woman to give birth on a plane; b) first stewardess; c) first woman pilot of a mail plane; or d) inventor of the altimeter.

51. Best Sellers and Standing Room Only

Match the author and the opus:

1. *Babbitt*	a) Liam O'Flaherty
2. *Buddenbrooks*	b) Sidney Kingsley
3. *The Last Tycoon*	c) Sinclair Lewis
4. *Ulysses*	d) Maxwell Anderson
5. *The Bridge of San Luis Rey*	e) Thomas Mann
6. *The Informer*	f) Sean O'Casey
7. *The Emperor Jones*	g) James Joyce
8. *The Plough and The Stars*	h) F. Scott Fitzgerald
9. *Dead End*	i) Eugene O'Neill
10. *Winterset*	j) Thornton Wilder

52. Cinema Classifieds

Lurking in these classified advertisements are descriptions of ten popular movies. Can you link up movies and ads?

BOX a) *Nightmare Alley*
    b) *The Fountainhead*
    c) *Kings Row*
    d) *The Best Years of Our Lives*
    e) *A Phantom Lady*
    f) *Gaslight*
    g) *Christmas Holiday*
    h) *The Big Clock*
    i) *The Unsuspected*
    j) *Double Indemnity*

LOST & FOUND
1. Found: one almost-burned pair of blood-stained trousers. If R. would claim them, perhaps we can come to a mutually beneficial arrangement. Abigail knows of this ad. Box ——.

PERSONALS
2. If the woman in the strange hat whom I met in a bar where "I Remember April" was being played will answer this ad, she may save my life. Box ——.

3. Lawyer urgently needed in medical malpractice suit. Have evidence proving my physician cut off my legs without cause. Box ——.

ANNOUNCEMENTS
4. Stop Crime on Radio. Society for prevention of Victor Grandison's crime broadcasts will meet in his niece's mansion. Box ——.

5. Unsecured loans. I'll lend money to honest farmers, if they're war vets. No collateral needed. Cornbelt Trust Co., Boone City. Box ——.

6. Carnival in Town. See Zeena, the carny queen; Mrs. Peabody, the occultist; and the Geek (it eats live chickens). Box ——.

7. Life Insurance. Nobody has enough insurance. Make sure you're protected now. Call Walter Neff Insurance, and ask about our special benefits clause. Box ——.

MERCHANDISE FOR SALE
8. For sale: portrait of the Empress Theodora of Byzantium. Has a sparkling beauty all its own. Apply the Alquist mansion. Box ——.

HELP WANTED
9. Publisher. To take over management of the Janoth magazines. Must be able to command trust of his editors. Box ——.

10. Architect. With training in newest ideas. Must be able to please architectural critics. Apply the Winand Building. Box ——.

53. Uh, Uh, Uh...Don't Touch That Dial!

1. How were the top songs picked on "Your Hit Parade"?

_____

2. What was the name of your host on "Inner Sanctum"? And who sponsored the show?

3. Who urged you to wake up, because it was time to stump the experts?

_____

4. Who conducted both "The Good Will Court" and "The Mediation Board"?

_____

5. What program featured a Manhattan detective who lived in a townhouse from where he rarely budged? (Hint: his hobbies were raising rare orchids and eating rare dishes.)

_____

6. Who was the Amicus Curiae?

_____

7. Who was the Town Crier?

_____

8. Jackie Kelk played Homer Brown in a situation comedy. What was its name? What actor played the lead?

_____

9. "Two Guitars" was the theme of this program. Harry Horlick's orchestra supplied the music. What was the name of the show?

_____

10. "You would look nice, your face would feel as cool as ice," if you took whose advice?

54. Taking Stock

✑ ✑ ✑ ✑ ✑ ✑

1. What business organization operated the "The Great White Fleet"?

_____

2. What railroad advertised that it "carried more passengers and handled more freight than any other railroad in America"?

_____

3. In what industries were the following men considered powerful: a) Col. William C. Procter; b) Edward A. Filene; c) Adolph Zukor?

_____

4. W. C. Durant and Jesse Livermore were well-known stock market operators. How did they differ in method?

_____

5. Who was Samuel Insull?

_____

6. Identify: a) Rit; b) Pointex; c) Pebeco.

_____

7. What were the twins who advertised a cleaning powder?

_____

8. What was Joseph C. Leyendecker's great claim to advertising fame?

9. What product was advertised by "Sunny Jim"?

─────────────

10. What product was advertised by a series of cartoons showing a man's head with fewer hairs in each successive panel, coupled with the slogan: "─────── will save it"?

55. They're Playing Our Song

Match the artists and the songs they made famous:

1. Eddie Fisher		a)	"Mam'selle"
2. Tennessee Ernie Ford and Kay Starr		b)	"Any Time"
3. Harmonicats		c)	"My Truly, Truly Fair"
4. Harry James		d)	"Mule Train"
5. Spike Jones		e)	"I'll Never Be Free"
6. Kay Kyser		f)	"Sugar Blues"
7. Frankie Laine		g)	"Peg O'My Heart"
8. Peggy Lee		h)	"A Shanty in Old Shanty Town"
9. Johnny Long		i)	"You Always Hurt the One You Love"
10. Art Lund		j)	"I Had the Craziest Dream"
11. Tony Martin		k)	"Mairzy Doats"
12. Clyde McCoy		l)	"Der Fuehrer's Face"
13. Merry Macs		m)	"Mañana"
14. Mills Brothers		n)	"To Each His Own"
15. Guy Mitchell		o)	"Three Little Fishes"

56. Starry Disguise

Try to match the star who played the star in the filmed biography:

SUBJECT	IMPERSONATOR
1. Marjorie Lawrence	a) James Cagney
2. Harry Houdini	b) Kirk Douglas
3. Red Nichols	c) Bob Hope
4. Grace Moore	d) Tony Curtis
5. Marilyn Miller	e) Eleanor Parker
6. Eddie Foy	f) June Haver
7. Ruth Etting	g) Alice Faye
8. Lillian Russell	h) Danny Kaye
9. Lon Chaney	i) Kathryn Grayson
10. Bix Beiderbecke	j) Doris Day

57. It's All Coming Back Now

1. Who was "Miraculous" Butler?

_____

2. What was the name and breed of FDR's dog?

3. Lindy was the first to solo nonstop from New York to Paris . . . but why?

4. Butterine was: a) artificial butter; b) the substance in goldenrod that caused hayfever; c) a soft coal; or d) a sulfa drug?

5. What animal was brought to America by Ruth Harkness in 1937?

6. Who submitted a 5-page paper, "Einheitlichen Feldtheorie," to the Prussian Academy of Sciences in 1929: a) Joseph Goebbels; b) Thomas Mann; c) Albert Einstein; d) Fritz Lang; or e) Marlene Dietrich?

7. Why did people say goodbye to "Hello, Central" in 1920?

8. For what accomplishment did Dr. Frederick Grant Banting receive the Nobel Prize?

9. Do you remember the popular expression coined by FDR on April 7, 1932? It later became part of the title of a song sung by Joan Blondell in *Gold Diggers of 1933*.

10. Who said "Every man is a king"?

58. The Talkies

Identify the movie from the meaningful squibs below:

1. "Is this the end of Rico?"

_____

2. "In a few moments now, I shall know why all this had to be."

_____

3. "We'll start with a few murders. Big men. Little men. Just to show we make no distinction . . . Even the moon is frightened of me, frightened to death."

_____

4. "You're wiser than anything on Earth. Look at me and see that I'm trying to help you!"

_____

5. "And the Beast looked upon the face of Beauty and lo! his hand was stayed from killing and from that day forward he was as one dead."

_____

6. "I know how much that meant to you, Mrs. Hamilton." . . . "I tol' him you was prostrate with grief." . . . "Dare I name it? Can it be love?"

_____

7. "But how do you get along; how do you live?" . . . "I steal."

8. "When you're slapped you'll take it and like it" . . . "By Gad, sir, you ARE a character!" . . . "I tell you right out, sir, I'm a man who likes talking to a man who likes to talk!"

---

9. "They call her 'Spot White'" . . . "It should be 'Spot Cash'!"

---

10. "I gave you a haircut three days ago and you were having a party then." . . . "Same party."

59. Soda Jerking

Translate these counter terms into English:

1. "pop boy"	a) lemon phosphate
2. "98"	b) banana split
3. "tamper"	c) whipped cream
4. "spla"	d) coffee soda with coffee and chocolate syrup
5. "hail"	e) incompetent soda jerk
6. "spiker"	f) ice in a drink
7. "black and white"	g) assistant manager
8. "Broadway"	h) chocolate malted with vanilla ice cream
9. "black cow"	i) ice pounder
10. "houseboat"	j) chocolate milk shake

60. Picassos of the Pulps

Match the cartoonists with their comic strips:

1. "Blondie"   a) Chester Gould
2. "The Timid Soul"   b) Sidney Smith
3. "Joe Palooka"   c) Hal Foster
4. "Henry"   d) Chic Young
5. "Terry and the Pirates"   e) Fontaine Fox
6. "Dick Tracy"   f) Harold T. Webster
7. "Red Ryder"   g) Rudolph Dirks
8. "Little Nemo"   h) Bud Fisher
9. "Happy Hooligan"   i) Ham Fisher
10. "Krazy Kat"   j) Carl Anderson
11. "Toonerville Folks"   k) George Herriman
12. "Mutt and Jeff"   l) Milton Caniff
13. "The Katzenjammer Kids"   m) Frederick Burr Opper
14. "Prince Valiant"   n) Windsor McCay
15. "The Gumps"   o) Fred Harman

61. Pick the Picture

How many of these movies can you identify?

1. An international killer returns home with a plastic surgeon who has changed his face.

2. A hard-working lady editor of a fashion magazine gets herself psychoanalyzed.

---

3. Greta Garbo plays a ballet dancer, John Barrymore is a no-account baron, and Joan Crawford is a stenographer.

---

4. A theremin hums a beautiful background theme while Waldo Lydecker does the killing.

---

5. Lord Horfield, the hanging judge, compares walnuts to the human brain in this Hitchcock classic.

---

6. Bigger Thomas accidentally smothers a white girl.

---

7. A decadent Rumanian blackmails a German underground fighter.

---

8. An ex-serviceman throws his tramp wife and her friends out of his apartment and is later suspected of her murder.

---

9. Three strangers meet on the Chinese New Year, invoke the aid of the Chinese goddess of luck to win the Irish Sweepstakes, and finally lose everything they have.

---

10. "Leslie . . . Leslie . . ." echoes through the bayous in an attempt to drive a shipwreck victim insane.

62. Quote Query

Who said:

1. "You ain't heard nothing yet, folks."

_____

2. "Gentlemen always seem to remember blondes."

_____

3. "Men seldom make passes
    At girls who wear glasses."

_____

4. "Believe it or not."

_____

5. "Beulah, peel me a grape."

_____

6. "The Era of Wonderful Nonsense."

_____

7. "I have found it impossible to carry the heavy burden of responsibility and to discharge my duties as King as I would wish to do without the help and support of the woman I love."

_____

8. "I should of stood in bed."

9. "Mad dogs and Englishmen go out in the mid-day sun."

10. "I want to be alone."

63. When Eddie Cantor Played Maxie the Taxie

1. Who was the MC of "Back That Fact"?

2. Can you name both of Ray Bolger's TV series?

3. Name all four of Sid Caesar's TV wives.

4. Who was Our Miss Brooks?

5. Who was The Man Against Crime?

6. Who was the ever-faithful executive secretary to the mysterious billionaire, John Beresford Tipton?

7. Who said: a) "Ten-four"; b) "I Love The Waad Open Spaces"; c) "Peace"?

8. What did all these actors have in common: Peter Falk, Richard Crenna, Edmond O'Brien, James Whitmore, and E. G. Marshall?

9. How did Imogene Coca, Shirley Booth, and Louise Beavers make their TV situation comedy livings?

10. Every summer, Mike Stokey would fill in for a regular TV show. What was the name of his perennial summer show?

64. Reading and Writing

1. In what books do the following characters appear: a) Kim Ravenal; b) Lady Ashley; c) Carol Kennicott?

2. Eugene O'Neill's middle name was a) Patrick; b) George; c) William; d) Gladstone.

3. In the 20s, the people having the most fun were known as "flaming youth." Where was this expression first used?

4. What do the initials in H. G. Wells's name stand for: a) Horatio Guthrie; b) Herbert George; c) Henry Gordon; or d) Harold Gardner?

5. Who wrote books about the Lawrenceville School and Dink Stover at Yale?

6. In what states are the following mythical places located, and who put them there: a) Gibbsville; b) Little Egg; c) Yoknapatawpha County; d) Zenith?

7. *Bella, Bella Kissed a Fella* was a book about a girl from The Bronx. Who wrote it?

8. Samuel Hopkins Adams wrote a novel about the scandals of the Harding Administration. What was its name?

9. What city was *Main Street* actually set in?

10. What was "My Day"?

65. Gilt-Edged Phrases

Remember the products these slogans advertised?—Most of them are still around!

1. "Cover the Earth"

_____

2. "The flavor lasts"

_____

3. "Good to the last drop"

_____

4. "When better cars are built, ———— will build them."

_____

5. "The candy mint with the hole"

_____

6. "The one cigarette sold the world over"

_____

7. "They work while you sleep"

_____

8. "Such popularity must be deserved"

_____

9. "It's toasted"

66. Just in Time

1. The 1929 income tax rate on the first $7,500 of income was: a) 1½%; b) 2½%; c) 4%; d) 5%.

2. The Pierce Arrow in 1929 was priced at: a) $2,000; b) $3,750; c) $4,000; d) $5,875.

3. In late 1936, the number "8" was on everybody's lips. Why?

4. When Edward VIII abdicated, he became the Duke of Windsor. What was his title before he became king? And what was his brother's title before *he* became king?

5. What state was the setting for Orson Welles's radio adaptation of *The War of the Worlds*?

6. When did the United States recognize the Soviet Union: a) 1917; b) 1929; c) 1933; d) 1941; e) 1945?

7. Define: a) crooning; b) swooning; c) snood.

8. When you received a letter with a list of ten names, you were to send a dime to the name on the top, add your name at the bottom, and send the letter to ten of your friends. If everyone kept sending the list to ten friends, each of whom sent it to ten friends, everyone would get rich. What was this scheme called?

9. What was the guessing game where you made motions with your hands and your friends had to guess what they represented?

10. Who was the insect friend of Pinocchio?

67. Field Day

1. In the Interscholastic Championships of 1933, a Cleveland high school track star tied the world record in the 100-yard dash, broke the interscholastic record in the 220, and won the broad jump by setting a 24-foot, 9⅝-inch record. Who was he?

2. The Augusta National was opened in 1933. Planned by one of golf's greatest names, it contained only 22 traps. Who designed it?

_____

3. What did these men have in common: Abe Simon, Gus Dorazio, Tony Musto?

_____

4. Who was the Galloping Ghost?

_____

5. Who were the Original Celtics?

_____

6. Who lost five times in his bid for the America's Cup?

_____

7. "Big Red" weighed 1,375 pounds and won 20 out of 21 races. What was his real name?

_____

8. Name the Four Horsemen.

_____

9. Who was "The Norwegian Doll"?

_____

10. What position did Bronco Nagurski play?

68. Loitering in the Lobby

𝒟 𝒟 𝒟 𝒟 𝒟 𝒟

1. Who was the composer of the theme music for *The Informer, King Kong,* and *Gone With The Wind*?

_____

2. Who played Sam Spade in the 1931 version of *The Maltese Falcon*?

_____

3. What story was *All That Money Can Buy* taken from?

_____

4. Complete these Betty Hutton movie titles: a) *The _____ In*; b) _____ *My Heart*; c) *The Miracle of _____*; d) *Here Come the _____*; e) *And the _____ Sing*.

_____

5. In what Marx Brothers movies did the following occur: a) Groucho's land auction; b) Harpo's mixup with passports and puppets; c) the stateroom scene; d) Harpo and Chico's bridge game?

_____

6. Who played the dumbbell second lead of the Dead End Kids and the Bowery Boys?

_____

7. Who usually played harassed, kindly fathers (*Meet Me in St. Louis, Little Women*)?

8. Judge Roy Bean in the TV series was played by a character actor who specialized in bearded old-timers. What was his name?

9. Scott Brady is to Lawrence Tierney as James Parrott was to ———.

10. Norma Shearer said these lines in what film: "That will be all, thank you" . . . "A new kind of man, a new kind of world"?

69. Radio Riddles

1. Who surprised the kiddies of his city by reading the comic strips to them in 1945?

2. A speeding bullet and a locomotive hopelessly competed with what hero?

3. Who told you to "take it or leave it"?

4. Who urged his horse on with these words: "Roll, Thunder, roll!"?

5. What show featured Joel Kupperman and Vanessa Brown?

6. Can you remember the real names of the Green Arrow and the Green Hornet?

7. How were the Lone Ranger and the Green Hornet related?

8. Who were Fran Striker and George W. Trendle?

9. Clem Kadiddlehopper is associated with what entertainer?

10. Who "rides on and lives on in the heart and the imagination of the world"?

70. Popping Some Popcorn Questions

ℐ ℐ ℐ ℐ ℐ ℐ

1. Richard Addinsell wrote what famous melody for *Dangerous Moonlight*?

2. You may have seen all four versions of the James Barrie comedy, *The Admirable Crichton*. Can you remember at least one version masquerading under another name?

3. Who was the MGM costume designer, married to Janet Gaynor, responsible for the square-shouldered dresses of the 40s?

4. Humph and Katie starred in *The African Queen*. John Huston directed it. Who were responsible for the original book and scenario?

5. Who were the subjects of the aviation biopix: a) *They Flew Alone*; b) *Flight for Freedom*; c) *Captain Eddie*; d) *Reach for The Sky*?

6. What was Warner Brothers' answer to the MGM Pete Smith shorts?

7. Name the Three Stooges.

8. George Marshall directed two versions of the same film twelve years apart. In 1952, he directed *Scared Stiff* with Dean Martin and Jerry Lewis. What was the name of the first version and who starred in it?

9. Who was the unbilled star who delivered the Maltese Falcon to Humphrey Bogart?

10. What do all these actors have in common: George Kuwa, Kamiyama Sojin, E. L. Park, Warner Oland, Sidney Toler, and Roland Winters?

71. Name Dropping

Fill in the names of these celebrities of the 40s:

1. Max and Buddy _____
2. Governor Ellis _____ of Georgia
3. Senator _____ Barkley
4. Congressman _____ Bloom
5. _____ Bush
6. _____ Chennault
7. _____ Clapper
8. Wild Bill _____
9. Hamilton _____
10. Carter _____
11. _____ Henderson
12. _____ Hillman
13. Cordell _____
14. _____ Laval
15. _____ Marcantonio
16. _____ Lee
17. _____ W. Nimitz
18. _____ Rosenman
19. _____ Sarazen
20. _____ Thornhill

72. Ladies with a Past

1. Where did Aimée Semple McPherson hold her revival meetings?

_____

2. Who wrote *The Turquoise*?

_____

3. The Duke and Duchess of York had two daughters. Can you name them?

_____

4. Who played Agatha Reed in a) the stage version of *Goodbye, My Fancy*; b) the movie?

_____

5. Who played Georgie Elgin in *The Country Girl*?

_____

6. Who was the screen star who married the Marquis de la Falaise de la Coudraye?

_____

7. What was the name of Betty Smith's novel about a New York City neighborhood?

_____

8. Name two ice skating champions who went into the movies.

9. Who was the first woman to swim the English Channel?

10. She was with The Pied Pipers and married bandleader Paul Weston. She and Frank Sinatra cut such records as "I'll Never Smile Again," "Whispering," and "The One I Love." Her name?

73. "Hey, Put Those Lights Out!"

𝒯 𝒯 𝒯 𝒯 𝒯 𝒯

1. Where did you find Minute Men during World War II?

2. Translate: a) kamikaze; b) banzai; c) Mikado; d) harakari; e) Bushido; f) samurai.

3. The two most important accomplishments of the Manhattan Project never took place in Manhattan. Where did they occur?

4. Three dots and a dash stood for "vitezsvi" in Czech. What did it stand for in English?

5. It cost $500 million, was made of 1.6 million cubic yards of concrete, 50,000 tons of steel plate, and it stretched 125 miles. What was it?

6. What was the destroyer USS *Ward* famous for?

7. Mt. Suribachi is located on what island? Who took the photo of the raising of the American flag there?

8. What were the "Four Freedoms"?

9. Identify the man who jumped from a Messerschmitt onto the grounds of Dungavel castle.

10. Who were Petain, Darlan, and Laval?

74. Movie Musicals

1. What was the movie musical that had a heel as the hero?

_____

2. Who was the Brazilian Bombshell?

_____

3. Who was the female lead in these movies: *Million Dollar Legs, Down Argentine Way, Moon Over Miami,* and *Pin Up Girl?*

_____

4. Who was the deadpan singer featured in *Ship Ahoy, The Harvey Girls,* and *Till the Clouds Roll By?*

_____

5. As Jeanette MacDonald looked out her train window in *Monte Carlo,* what song did she sing?

_____

6. Who starred in *Thanks a Million, Love Thy Neighbor, It's In The Bag,* and *Full House?*

_____

7. Gene Kelly danced with a mouse in what picture?

_____

8. Who were Patty, Maxine, and La Verne?

_____

9. What was the first all-talkie produced by Warner Bros.?

10. Bebe Daniels broke her leg in what movie?

75. Law and Order

1. In 1923, the President of the Black Star Line was tried in Federal Court for using the mails to defraud. Who was he?

2. Minnesota Congressman Andrew J. Volstead's act was passed in 1919. What did it do?

3. What was the Sick Chicken Case?

4. A muscular corset salesman murdered a middle-aged art editor, assisted by the victim's wife. Gruesome details included poisoned whiskey, skull smashing, and a $100,000 insurance policy. What murder case was this?

5. Who was the first cabinet member convicted as a felon?

6. In 1933, Pelican Island was transferred to the Department of Justice. What did this mean to the nation's toughest criminals?

7. The ex-governor of New York and President of the American Bar Association who prosecuted Police Lt. Becker for the Rosenthal murder was: a) Walt Whitman; b) Charles S. Whitman; c) Herbert Lehman; d) Thomas E. Dewey.

8. For the murder of a Massachusetts paymaster, these two men were convicted and executed, creating an uproar among liberals and intellectuals. What were their names?

9. What made the shooting of six gangsters in Bugs Moran's garage so memorable?

10. When Utah became the thirty-sixth state to ratify the 21st Amendment, what happened?

76. Fun and Games

1. What was the all-inclusive term given the coconut shells, rattles, tin whistles, etc., used by a jazz drummer?

2. Can you name three card games that emphasized melds?

3. If you skirt the big thruways and take older, quieter roads, you may still come across the remains of a national craze of the 30s—a stunted version of an ancient and honorable sport. What was its name?

4. What was the ancient Filipino toy that took America by storm in 1929 and returns every year to capture a new generation?

5. Do you move clockwise or counterclockwise in Monopoly?

6. How many strings on a uke?

7. What was everybody doing in the song, "Everybody's Doing It"?

8. What did the girl lose in the song, "She Had to Go And Lose It at The Astor"?

9. Who wrote "Will You Love Me in December as You Do in May"?

10. What's the gadget you hold when using a Ouija board?

77. Sell and Tell

    🍃 🍃 🍃 🍃 🍃 🍃 🍃

1. What foiled Peter Pain again and again?

_____

2. What brand of ginger ale was advertised by an Eskimo band?

_____

3. What did "Spotless Town" verses advertise?

_____

4. What product said it was "time to re-tire"?

_____

5. What is "99 and 44/100% pure"?

_____

6. What pipe tobacco was sold in "tidy red tins"?

_____

7. What was the "food shot from guns"?

_____

8. Complete the following: "If it's safe in water, it's safe in ——."

_____

9. What were advertised as being "Orthophonic"?

_____

10. What "ruled the waves"?

78. Accounting for the Time

1. The tranquil Bahamas in the 40s were the scene of a fascinating, still uncleared-up murder case. Who was murdered?

_____

2. "We have introduced the element of surprise in dealing with burglars," said Herbert Hoover at the 50th anniversary of this invention. What invention was it?

_____

3. In 1941, Bulova Watch sponsored an NBC special for only $12.00. The price was right, since only 4,500 Americans could enjoy it. Why?

_____

4. What was "The Living Newspaper"?

_____

5. What was the Ashcan School?

_____

6. Dick Calkins and Phil Nolan thought up the idea. Buster Crabbe was the hero. What was the name of the serial?

_____

7. What was Joey Chill's infamous crime?

8. Gopher Prairie was created by what author?

9. Who played Annie Oakley in *Annie Get Your Gun*: a) on Broadway; b) in the movies?

10. What was Willy Loman's job?

79. Bird Men

ℐ ℐ ℐ ℐ ℐ ℐ ℐ

1. Lindberg flew across the Atlantic in: a) 10 hours; b) 15½ hours; c) 25 hours, 10 minutes; d) 33 hours, 29 minutes; e) 45 hours, 52 minutes.

2. What was the original airmail rate when airmail was established on May 15, 1918: a) 5¢ an ounce; b) 8¢ an ounce; c) 15¢ an ounce; d) 24¢ an ounce; e) $1.00 an ounce?

3. To whom was Pilot License #1 issued: a) Eddie Rickenbacker; b) President Woodrow Wilson; c) Glenn Curtiss; d) Orville and Wilbur Wright; e) Black Jack Pershing?

4. What rank did Charles A. Lindbergh hold during World War I?

5. Who mistakenly piloted "The Flying Crate" to Ireland?

6. What part of a balloon was the nacelle?

7. What did all these have in common: Liberty, Packard, Curtiss, Wright, Lawrence?

8. What was the name of the airplane in which Richard E. Byrd crossed the Atlantic: a) The Lindy; b) Virginia Dare; c) America; d) The North Star; e) Polaris?

9. Did the *Graf Zeppelin* ever circle the globe?

10. What was the name of the dirigible lost at Lakehurst, N. J., in 1937?

80. Early Movies

1. Who directed *The Covered Wagon?*

_____

2. What movie comic was married to Natalie Talmadge?

_____

3. What actress with the initials MMM made her first screen appearance in 1915?

_____

4. In what films did Douglas Fairbanks: a) capture a ship singlehandedly; b) use a long whip; c) take a trip on a flying carpet?

_____

5. What actress played opposite Rudolph Valentino in *The Sheik?*

_____

6. Give the first names of the Farnum brothers.

_____

7. What dancer from *Chin Chin* and *The Follies* became a movie star and a great and good friend of a publisher?

_____

8. *Passion* introduced what star to American audiences?

9. Who starred in *Madame X* and *Zaza*?

10. What was the name of Valentino's last picture?

81. Driving Home the Answers

1. When did the Model A supersede the Model T: a) 1918; b) 1927; c) 1929; d) 1935?

2. What did all these have in common: Alco, Pope-Toledo, Lozier, Thomas, Chandler?

3. In 1926, Ab Jenkins drove from New York City to San Francisco. What was his approximate time: a) 75 hours; b) 86 hours; c) 5 days; d) 181 hours?

4. What was the platform you used to mount to get into a car?

5. Salesmen most often drove: a) roadsters; b) flivvers; c) coupes; d) jitneys.

6. Who produced the 1936 Terraplane?

7. Who produced the Airflow?

8. What car was promoted with ads headlined: "Somewhere West of Laramie"?

9. What car was promoted with ads headlined: "The Price of Leadership"?

10. What did Socony stand for?

82. Listening Under the Covers

1. Why did the Lone Ranger carry on a personal vendetta against the Hole-in-the-Wall gang and its despicable chief? Do you remember the chief's name?

2. Who used to say, "What a revolting development this is!"?

_____

3. Can you remember who headed up these four crime-fighting groups: a) Secret Guard; b) SBI; c) Counterspies; d) Secret Squadron?

_____

4. Who used to call out, "Uga Uga Boo, A Boo Boo Uga!"?

_____

5. Who impatiently said, "All right, all right."?

_____

6. No president ever served more than four terms, but one radio actor played scores of presidents. Who was he?

_____

7. Who were the three sleuths in "I Love A Mystery"?

_____

8. What did "The Adventures of Helen and Mary" change its name to?

_____

9. Denny was the assistant of a) Mr. Keen; b) Bulldog Drummond; c) Sam Spade; d) Hearthstone of the Death Squad?

_____

10. Who were the six tenants of Allen's Alley?

83. Counter Calls

Can you make sense out of these soda fountain orders?

1.	"burn one"	a)	boss is around
2.	"burn one all the way"	b)	customer walking out without paying
3.	"draw one"	c)	"burn one," with chocolate ice cream
4.	"shoot one"	d)	cup of coffee
5.	"86"	e)	syrup
6.	"95"	f)	all out of the item ordered
7.	"Pittsburgh"	g)	pineapple syrup
8.	"13"	h)	chocolate malted milk
9.	"Chicago"	i)	toast is burning
10.	"goo"	j)	Coca-Cola

84. Movie Mysteries

1. "It took more than one man to change my name to Shanghai Lily," she told Captain Harvey, in *Shanghai Express*. Who played Shanghai Lily and Captain Harvey?

2. George Eastman rowed Alice Tripp across Loon Lake in *A Place in The Sun*. Who played George Eastman and Alice Tripp?

3. "Tangerine" was heard in the background as Phyllis Dietrichson and Walter Neff shot each other in *Double Indemnity*. Who played these parts?

4. Who played Frankenstein in the 1931 Universal production?

5. Who "invented": a) the submachine gun; b) the light bulb; c) the carbine rifle; d) laughing gas?

6. Who wore a "peek-a-boo bang"?

7. Ezra Stone played Henry Aldrich on radio. Who played him in the movies?

8. Who were the three acting sisters who appeared in *Four Daughters, Four Wives,* and *Four Mothers*?

9. Who played the native dancer and the Red Shadow in Sigmund Romberg's *Desert Song*?

10. Who played Charlie Chan's #2 son?

85. Newsstand

1. Name the founder-publishers of the *Reader's Digest*.

_____

2. Henry Ford's excursion into publishing proved embarrassing to him. What was his journal?

_____

3. Alumni and undergrads of which colleges read the following humor magazine: a) *Record*; b) *Chapparal*; c) *Gargoyle*; d) *Lampoon*?

_____

4. *Judge* and *Life* were two of the three big humor magazines forty years ago. What was the third?

_____

5. To what city would you have sent a letter to the editor of: a) *The Saturday Evening Post*; b) *Collier's*; c) *Youth's Companion*; d) *The Red Book*?

86. Cole Porter Quiz

1. Fred Astaire and Ginger Rogers starred in this 1934 adaptation of a Porter musical. Just one song—"Night and Day"—was used from the original Broadway score, and another composer's song—"The Continental"—won an Oscar. Name this un-Porterish Porter movie.

_____

2. Some of the songs from this musical, which featured William Gaxton, Victor Moore, and Ethel Merman, included "I Get a Kick Out of You," "All Through the Night," "You're the Top," and "Blow, Gabriel, Blow." What was the show?

_____

3. A 1935 Porter musical—which had Montgomery Clift as an unfeatured player—tried to introduce a newfangled dance to ballrooms. What was the song which celebrated this dance?

_____

4. Who played Cole Porter in the biopic, _Night and Day_?

_____

5. Remember this movie with Eleanor Powell, James Stewart, and Virginia Bruce? You heard "I've Got You Under My Skin" and "It's De-Lovely" in it.

_____

6. Who sang "My Heart Belongs to Daddy" in _Leave It To Me_?

7. Who starred in: a) *Du Barry Was a Lady*; b) *Let's Face It*; c) *Something to Shout About*?

8. Much to the surprise of the composer, Roy Rogers sang this song in *Hollywood Canteen*. It later become a hit. What was the name of this uncharacteristic Porter melody?

9. *Kiss Me, Kate* had over one thousand performances. Its songs included "Why Can't You Behave?" "So In Love," "Wunderbar," "Were Thine That Special Face," and "Always True to You in My Fashion." How many of the featured stars can you remember?

10. "Farewell, Amanda" was heard in a delightful 1949 film that starred Hepburn and Tracy. What was its name?

87. Auld Lang Syne

1. Why was Mayor La Guardia of New York City called The Little Flower?

2. What are the five points of the Girl Scouts?

---

3. What President first spoke over the radio: a) Wilson, 1916; b) Harding, 1923; c) Hoover, 1931; d) Roosevelt, 1933?

---

4. Which country did not belong to the League of Nations: a) Russia; b) Italy; c) U.S.A.; d) France?

---

5. Why did John D. Rockefeller always give away a brand-new dime?

---

6. Which country did not sign the 10-year Rome Peace Pact (July 15, 1933): a) Poland; b) Italy; c) France; d) Germany; e) England?

---

7. What was the average bonus paid to veterans in 1936: a) $100; b) $440; c) $550; d) $1,000; e) $2,000?

---

8. Complete the dance names: a) Big ———; b) Lambeth ———; c) Black ———; d) Lindy ———.

---

9. The University of Winnemac and the McGurk Institute are two of the settings of this 1924 novel by Sinclair Lewis. Name it.

---

10. Whose name is associated with the Single Tax scheme?

88. Movies Gone By

1. The three major Oscar winners in 1938 were all repeaters. Best actress won her first Oscar for *Dangerous*, her second for *Jezebel*; best actor won his first for *Captains Courageous*, his second for *Boys Town*; best director won his first for *It Happened One Night*, his second for *Mr. Deeds Goes to Town*, his third for *You Can't Take It With You*. Who were these Hollywood giants?

———————

2. In the original *Goodbye Mr. Chips*, Robert Donat was the schoolmaster. Who played Mrs. Chips, in her first movie role?

———————

3. A wirehaired terrier named Asta delighted moviegoers in what detective series?

———————

4. Hitchcock's not the only director who likes to get into the act. Name the directors who were seen in these movies they directed: a) *Sullivan's Travels*; b) *The Treasure of the Sierra Madre*.

———————

5. In what movie did you first hear the word "pixilated"?

———————

6. Identify the acting brother of: a) Tom Conway; b) Peter Graves; c) Arthur Shields.

———————

7. How many members of Our Gang can you name?

8. *White Christmas* and *A Christmas Carol* are only two of the many Hollywood movies about Yuletide. Can you fill in the missing words from these Christmas movie titles: a) *The Holly and the* ———; b) *Tenth Avenue* ——— ———; c) ——— *on 34th Street*; d) *The Bishop's* ———; e) *Christmas in* ———.

9. Who brought 'em back alive?

10. What famed German actor was born in Brooklyn?

89. Bands and Vocalists

1. Complete the names of these studio bands: a) Harry Horlick and the ———; b) Sam Lanin and the ———; c) Harry Reser and the ———.

2. Name the bands most associated with these singers: a) Merv Griffin; c) Mike Douglas; c) Eddy Howard; d) Don Cornell.

3. Girl singers often married their band leaders. Do you remember who married: a) Ozzie Nelson; b) Kay Kyser; c) Charlie Spivak; d) Raymond Scott; e) Stan Kenton; f) Boyd Raeburn?

4. What do these people have in common: Frank Parker, Lu Ann Sims, and Janette Davis?

5. Raleigh sponsored this show starring The Incomparable Hildegarde. Ted Weems and Harry Sosnik led the band. What was the show's name?

90. They've All Run Their Course

1. Who were the Black Knights' Mr. Inside and Mr. Outside?

2. Who was the only simultaneous 3-title boxing champ?

3. Why was Kenesaw Mountain Landis called the "czar"?

---

4. What was the "long count"?

---

5. He was 6'11" and weighed 280 lbs; his shoe size was 21½; his collars were size 24. What was his name?

---

6. In 1939 and 1940, this driver won the Indianapolis "500" in a Boyle Special. His name?

---

7. Who was known as "The Human Freight Car"?

---

8. Name the boxer who was deacon of a church and who recited the 144th Psalm before each fight.

---

9. What famous golfer was called "Long Jim"?

---

10. Howard and Robert excelled in what sport . . . and what was their last name?

91. Give Me An Old-Fashioned Slogan

Identify the products these advertising catchphrases made famous:

1. "The instrument of the immortals"
   _____

2. "They satisfy"
   _____

3. "A shilling in London, a quarter here"
   _____

4. "I'se in town, honey"
   _____

5. "Just a real good car"
   _____

6. "Ask Dad, he knows"
   _____

7. "Eventually, why not now?"
   _____

8. "Hasn't scratched yet"

9. "Have you a little fairy in your home?"

10. "A skin you love to touch"

92. Mismatched

Match the person with the object:

1. Gov. Ellis Arnall	a)	coming-out party
2. Hap Arnold	b)	a microphone
3. Danny Arnstein	c)	crown jewels
4. Thomas Hart Benton	d)	quints
5. Major Bowes	e)	airplanes
6. Allan Roy Dafoe	f)	oil painting
7. Marcel Duchamp	g)	a bell
8. Lady Elizabeth Bowes— Lyon	h)	Georgia peach
9. Brenda Diana Duff Frazier	i)	Burma Road
10. William Joyce (Lord Haw Haw)	j)	*Nude Descending a Staircase*

93. Comic Sidekicks

Leapin' Lizards! Just about every comic hero had a partner —usually a clod who was good for a laugh, but sometimes a friend in need. Bring hero and sidekick together.

1. Red Ryder		a)	Wash Tubbs
2. Captain America		b)	Connie
3. Plastic Man		c)	Roscoe Sweeney
4. Captain Midnight		d)	Speedy
5. Moon Mullins		e)	Toro
6. Archie Andrews		f)	Aqualad
7. Captain Easy		g)	Papoose
8. Terry		h)	Robin
9. Buz Sawyer		i)	Bucky
10. Don Winslow		j)	Woozy Winks
11. Mandrake the Magician		k)	Ichabod "Icky" Mudd
12. Batman		l)	Kayo
13. Green Arrow		m)	Lothar
14. Human Torch		n)	Jughead Jones
15. Aquaman		o)	Red Pennington

94. Motion Picture Archeology

1. Who did the voices for Bugs Bunny, Sylvester, and Tweetie Pie?

2. In fourteen years of MGM short stories, this Oscar winner and popular humorist specialized in complicating the simplest situations. What was his name?

3. What was Hope Emerson's most distinctive feature?

4. What did Donald Cook, Eddie Quillan, Ralph Bellamy, and William Gargan have in common?

5. What did Flora Robson, Bette Davis, Sarah Bernhardt, and Jean Simmons have in common?

6. Complete the titles of these Judy Garland pictures: a) *Thoroughbreds Don't* ———; b) *Every Sunday* ————; c) *Little Nellie* ———; d) *Babes on* ———; e) *Presenting Lily* ———.

7. Who was the great opera star Sam Goldwyn turned into a *silent* screen actress?

8. Edward Brophy played Goldie, the valet, in what series? Who played the lead?

9. *Weekend at the Waldorf* was the 1945 remake of ———?

10. Marlene Dietrich starred as Frenchy in this tragicomic western. Name the film.

95. Batting Champions

From the names below, give the batting champions in both leagues for the years asked for:

Luke Appling, Jimmy Fox, Joe DiMaggio, George Stirnweiss, Mickey Vernon, Buddy Myer, Lou Gehrig, Charlie Gehringer, Ted Williams, Lou Boudreau, Chuck Klein, Paul Waner, Arky Vaughan, Harry Walker, Dixie Walker, Stan Musial, Ernie Lombardi, Pete Reiser, Joe Medwick, Johnny Mize, Debs Garms, Phil Cavaretta

	YEAR	AMERICAN	NATIONAL
1.	1933		
2.	1934		
3.	1935		
4.	1936		
5.	1937		
6.	1938		
7.	1939		
8.	1940		
9.	1941		
10.	1942		
11.	1943		
12.	1944		
13.	1945		
14.	1946		
15.	1947		

96. Ancestral Memories

1. Who was the goat gland man?

_____

2. What do all these people have in common: Alex Wollcott, Harold Ross, Robert Benchley, Marc Connelly, Franklin P. Adams, Deems Taylor, George S. Kaufman, Dorothy Parker, and Robert E. Sherwood?

_____

3. Who said "When more and more people are thrown out of work, unemployment results"?

_____

4. What do all these people have in common: Burleigh Grimes, Charley Root, Eddie Rommel, Howard Ehmke, and Urban Faber?

_____

6. In 1929, *Miss America VIII* set a record of 75 mph to win the Harmworth Trophy. Who built her?

_____

6. What is the motto of the Boy Scouts?

_____

7. Where were many of Harold Bell Wright's novels set?

_____

8. What do all these have in common: Raymond & Whitcomb, Frank Co., Clark Co., and Gates Co.?

9. Name the author and his book in which Mark Sabre appeared.

_____

10. What was Hunter's *Biology*?

97. Past Pairs

Some famous people shared the same last name. Do you remember what those names were?

1. Golfer and government administrator: Bobby and Jesse_____

2. Band leader and plane builder: Freddie and Glen L. _____

3. Show business pair: Lorenz and Moss_____

4. Father and son movie figures: Walter and John _____

5. Novelist and propagandist: James and William——

6. Congressional Representatives: Jeannette and John _____

7. Dancer and celebrity: Gene and Shipwreck_____

8. Philosopher and actress: Bertrand and Rosalind _____

9. Novelists: Frank and Kathleen_____

10. Oilman and writer: Harry and Upton_____

98. Biopics

Match the performers and the historical characters they portrayed in the movies:

1. Edward G. Robinson		a)	Mme. Curie
2. Ginger Rogers		b)	Mme. Du Barry
3. Henry Fonda		c)	Paul Ehrlich
4. Ingrid Bergman		d)	Thomas Edison
5. Shepperd Strudwick		e)	Saint Bernadette
6. Frederic March		f)	Charlotte Brontë
7. Vivien Leigh		g)	Abraham Lincoln
8. Greer Garson		h)	Saint Joan
9. Olivia de Havilland		i)	Dolley Madison
10. Alexander Knox		j)	Edgar Allan Poe
11. Michael O'Shea		k)	Jack London
12. Jennifer Jones		l)	Mark Twain
13. Robert Walker		m)	Woodrow Wilson
14. Spencer Tracy		n)	Lady Emma Hamilton
15. Dolores Del Rio		o)	Robert Schumann

99. Antique Collection

1. What was the Republican party campaign song of 1936:
a) "We Are Coming, Father Abraham"; b) "O Susannah";
c) "Battle Hymn of the Republic"; d) "Alexander's Ragtime Band"?

2. In 1929 there was an uproar because of a threatened postage hike. What was the first-class rate then: a) 2¢; b) 3¢; c) 4¢?

3. What was an Army recruit's monthly pay in 1929: **a)** $21; b) $45; c) $55; d) $80?

4. The often weird headlines of *Variety,* the entertainment trade publication, have puzzled nonprofessionals down through the years. Can you translate: a) "Sticks Nix Hix Pix"; b) "Wall Street Lays An Egg"; c) "Blitz Boffs Buff Biz"?

5. What was the "Case of the Minister and the Choir Singer"?

6. In what year was cellophane invented: a) 1900; **b)** 1915; c) 1924; d) 1934?

7. What did all these people have in common: Ned Buntline, Kin Brady, and Nick Carter?

8. What did Graham McNamee and Major White have in common?

9. Who led the team bearing diphtheria serum to Nome?

10. Earl Browder was: a) Red Cross chairman; b) Communist leader; c) Republican party leader; d) Tory party leader who forced King Edward VIII to resign?

100. Medieval Movies

1. What movie director (*Variety, Atlantic, The Scarf*) once edited a great European newspaper?

2. Name all seven dwarfs.

3. Martin and Osa Johnson exhibited a film documentary in 1927. What was the subject?

4. What film comedian wore eyeglasses without lenses?

5. What movie director (*The Freshman*) was a former big-league baseball player?

6. What silent screen star had one blue eye and one brown eye?

7. What silent screen star (*The Big Parade, The Cossacks*) had been a circus bareback rider?

---

8. Jackie Gleason made this silent screen star (*Foolish Wives, Broken Barriers*) famous again. What was her name?

---

9. Who asked, "A-ah, what's up, Doc?"

---

10. Baby Dumpling was an important member of whose family?

101. Lapsed Slogans

Identify the product:

1. "Four out of five get it before they are 40"

---

2. "Chases dirt"

_____

3. "Keep that schoolgirl complexion"

_____

4. "Ask the man who owns one."

_____

5. "What a whale of a difference just a few cents makes"

_____

6. "We are advertised by our loving friends"

_____

7. "America's most famous dessert"

_____

8. "Children cry for it"

_____

9. "The nation's host from coast to coast"

_____

10. "High as the Alps in Quality"

102. Radio Echoes

℘ ℘ ℘ ℘ ℘ ℘

1. Identify these five "big" radio programs: a) a children's adventure show that told you "there's no school today"; b) a variety show that called everyone "dahling"; c) a soap opera with such characters as Ruth Evans Wayne, Nurse Burton, and Dr. John Wayne; d) a drama featuring newspapermen; and e) an adventure show with Steve Wilson, editor of *The Illustrated News*.

———

2. Who played the Bickering Bickersons, and who played John's brother, Amos?

———

3. Who conducted the Longines Symphonette? Who was the announcer?

———

4. "Lux Radio Theatre" featured radio rewrites of movies. Can you name any similar radio programs?

———

5. What did LS/MFT stand for?

———

6. Who conducted the Cities Service Band of America?

———

7. Charlie McCarthy was only one of Edgar Bergen's wooden-headed friends. Can you name any others?

8. If you had been the proud possessor of Hike-O-Meter, a Whistling Ring, a Secret Decoder, and a Norden Bombsight, you were either a master spy or a fan of which radio show?

9. Name two carbon copies of "First Nighter."

10. Where were you likely to hear: "Check and double check"; "I'se regusted"; "Ow wah! Ow wah!"; and "Buzz me, Miss Blue"?

103. Hollywood Revival

1. What movie actor played Scrooge annually on a Christmas Eve radio show?

2. This actress specialized in "name" films. Some of her pictures have been: *Captain Blood, Anthony Adverse, Adventures of Robin Hood, Princess O'Rourke,* and *My Cousin Rachel.* Her name?

3. *Flowers and Trees* was the first film in full technicolor. Who produced it?

4. What did George Arliss, Derrick de Marney, John Gielgud, and Alec Guinness have in common?

5. What movie actress's name means "Frosted Yellow Willow"?

6. Who rewrote Shaw's *Pygmalion* for the movies?

7. This daughter of a famous stage designer remembered mama . . . panicked in the streets . . . and was by love possessed. Her name?

8. What was the name of Mickey Mouse's girlfriend?

9. What did Mitzi Green and Ann Gillis have in common?

10. Identify these "one-name" stars: a) English ice-skater and dancer; b) a short French comic; c) a Mexican bullfighter-clown; d) a French model and actress.

104. Writer's Cramp

1. What book published annually was edited by Edward Joseph Harrington O'Brien?

_____

2. Who wrote *The Greatest Thing in the World?*

_____

3. What book did Margaret Mitchell write?

_____

4. Who wrote *The Gods Are Athirst* and *Penguin Island?*

_____

5. *North to the Orient* was the title of her first book. Her name?

_____

6. Who wrote the Burma Shave signs?

_____

7. For whom did Arthur Brisbane write editorials?

_____

8. What did these men have in common: Edward Hope, Keith Preston, Jake Falstaff, Ted Robinson, J. E. House, and Heywood Broun?

9. Name the magazines that had these departments: a) "The Lexicographer's Easy Chair"; b) "We Nominate for the Hall of Fame"; c) "Short Turns and Encores"; d) "The Contributor's Club"; e) "Americana"?

10. How did Paul de Kruif help Sinclair Lewis in the writing of *Arrowsmith*?

105. Raking Up the Past

1. In 1927 this sad leftover from history died. She had been an Archduchess at 17, an Empress at 23, and for 60 years, a madwoman. Who was she?

2. Who was talking about whom: "I could not help being charmed by his gentle, simple bearing and his calm, detached poise"?: a) Mussolini about Hitler; b) Wilson about the Kaiser; c) Churchill about Mussolini; d) the Duke of Windsor about Gandhi; e) Stalin about Lenin?

3. What a) Chief Justice, b) radical labor leader, c) sportsman, d) politico, were known as "Big Bill"?

_____

4. Who was Gluyas Williams?

_____

5. What did all these men have in common: Bert Savoy, Dave Montgomery, Joe Weber, Bobbie Clark?

_____

6. What was FPA's full name?

_____

7. What was Bing Crosby's real first name?

_____

8. Jimmy Doolittle set a first in September 1929 in a two-seat biplane. What did he do?

_____

9. Who said, "History is bunk"?

_____

10. Who was the Notre Dame football coach killed in an airplane crash in 1931?

106. Musical Movies

Match the movie musicals and their songs:

1. "Mammy"
2. "Tiptoe Through the Tulips"
3. "Louise"
4. "I'm an Indian"
5. "Am I Blue?"
6. "There's a Rainbow 'Round my Shoulder"
7. "Let's Face the Music and Dance"
8. "Chant of the Jungle"
9. "Happy Days Are Here Again"
10. "Sing You Sinners"

a) *Honey*
b) *Chasin' Rainbows*
c) *The Jazz Singer*
d) *Follow the Fleet*
e) *Gold Diggers of Broadway*
f) *Untamed*
g) *Innocents of Paris*
h) *The Singing Fool*
i) *My Man*
j) *On With The Show*

107. Is That the Blue Network, or the Red?

1. What was the story of an Iowa stenographer who fell in love with and married Broadway matinee idol Larry Noble?

2. You could become a "lemac" if you answered questions correctly on what show?

3. Name the panel, and the storytelling genius, on "Can You Top This?"

4. What program was dedicated to "The Three B's—Barrelhouse, Boogie-Woogie, and the Blues"?

5. Benjamin Ordway always returned "in exactly forty-seven seconds with the solution to tonight's case." What was his profession?

6. As the old morning bugle call of the covered wagons died away among the echoes, who told you another story of Death Valley Days?

7. " 'Jim is slim,' said Tim to Kim. 'Jim *is* slim, Tim,' to him said Kim." What quiz show featured these thought-twisters?

8. Who informed you that "This . . . is . . . London"?

9. What program was only based on a copyrighted book by Frederick L. Collins, and was "not an official program"? And who sponsored it?

10. This detective had to step on a drugstore scale to find out his weight and fortune. His fortune was danger. What was his weight . . . and his name?

108. World Series Winners

Who won the world series in:

1. 1933. The New York Giants or Washington Senators?
2. 1934. Detroit Tigers or St. Louis Cardinals?
3. 1935. Detroit Tigers or the Chicago Cubs?
4. 1936. N. Y. Giants or the N. Y. Yankees?
5. 1937. N. Y. Yankees or the N. Y. Giants?
6. 1938. Chicago Cubs or N. Y. Yankees?
7. 1939. N. Y. Yankees or the Cincinnati Reds?
8. 1940. Detroit Tigers or Cincinnati Reds?
9. 1941. N. Y. Yankees or the Brooklyn Dodgers?
10. 1942. St. Louis Cardinals or the N. Y. Yankees?
11. 1943. N. Y. Yankees or the St. Louis Cardinals?
12. 1944. St. Louis Browns or St. Louis Cardinals?
13. 1945. Detroit Tigers or the Chicago Cubs?
14. 1946. St. Louis Cardinals or the Boston Red Sox?
15. 1947. N. Y. Yankees or the Brooklyn Dodgers?

109. Turn That Radio Down!

1. Who knew of "Gh-o-o-st stories! Wierd stories! And murders, too!"?

2. What was the name of the Mystery Man in "The House of Mystery"?

_____

3. When the control tower heard, "CX-4"—who was coming in for a landing?

_____

4. What was "a dramatic story of human conflict vividly told from the point of view of someone closely involved"?

_____

5. George Shelton used to "work in that town." Who were his fellow panel-nuts on "It Pays to Be Ignorant"?

_____

6. Who spent most of his time in The Blue Note, talking to Ann Williams and the bartender, Ethelbert?

_____

7. What were Fred and Lucy Kent and their son dramatically struggling for?

_____

8. Who were the Halls of Ivy?

_____

9. You remember Gertrude Berg as Mrs. Goldberg. Do you know another serial she wrote and starred in?

_____

10. What early radio newsman spoke at a rate of 217 words per minute and wore a white patch over his left eye?

110. Casting Director

From the list on the right, pick the actor ideally suited to play the roles given on the left:

1. Henpecked husband with bald head, nervous twitches, frantic gestures
2. Historical figure, given to avuncular advice and bringing young lovers together
3. Fast-talking tough guy with heart of gold
4. A crazed hunchback
5. A sympathetic good guy
6. A dumb know-it-all
7. A portly butler
8. A crooked lawyer
9. A crooked sheriff
10. An excitable Italian

a) Erik Rhodes
b) Jack Carson
c) Leon Errol
d) Robert Greig
e) George Arliss
f) Barton MacLane
g) Brian Donlevy
h) Dwight Frye
i) MacDonald Carey
j) Samuel S. Hinds

111. Keep in Mind

1. Amelia Earhart died in an attempt to do what?

_____

2. To whom was the plea, "Say it ain't so, Joe," addressed?

3. Roy Chapman Andrews discovered the eggs of what creature in the Gobi?

---

4. Whose tomb in 1922 disclosed many riches?

---

5. Which Prime Minister of Poland was also an eminent concert pianist?

---

6. Hull House is associated with: Charles Francis Adams; b) Maude Adams; c) Sherwood Adams; d) Jane Addams.

---

7. Where is "St. John the Unfinished"?

---

8. In 1929, the University of Chicago appointed a 30-year-old as president. What was his name?

---

9. What was the pen name of Arthur Sarsfield Ward, author of the Fu Manchu stories?

---

10. Where did President Franklin D. Roosevelt die?

112. Commemorating the Comics

1. In what three comic books did Captain Marvel appear?

———————

2. What was the name of Billy Batson's valet?

———————

3. What was Billy Batson's job?

———————

4. *Planet*'s letters column was called what?

———————

5. Who were the members of the Monster Society of Evil?

———————

6. What did Captain Marvel's "SHAZAM" mean?

———————

7. Mary Batson also said "SHAZAM." She became Mary Marvel when she did so. What did *her* "SHAZAM" stand for?

———————

8. Name Dr. Sivana's brood.

———————

9. Superman had a large monogram on his chest. What did Captain Marvel wear on *his* chest?

0. Name two other comic strips appearing in the same omic book with Captain Marvel.

113. Two By Two

$\mathscr{D} \ \mathscr{D} \ \mathscr{D} \ \mathscr{D} \ \mathscr{D} \ \mathscr{D}$

air these acting teams:

1. Greta Garbo	a)	Charles Boyer
2. William Powell	b)	George Brent
3. Fred Astaire	c)	Olivia de Havilland
4. Donald O'Connor	d)	John Gilbert
5. Spencer Tracy	e)	Walter Pidgeon
6. Percy Kilbride	f)	Myrna Loy
7. Errol Flynn	g)	Katherine Hepburn
8. Bette Davis	h)	Ginger Rogers
9. Greer Garson	i)	Ann Blyth
0. Irene Dunne	j)	Marjorie Main

114. Radio Addresses

Match the radio show with its location:

1. A New York townhouse
2. A fix-it shop
3. Wheeling, W. Va.
4. Echo Valley Farm
5. Jonesport, Maine
6. A shop on Beacon Street
7. Tremont Avenue
8. 17 South Jackson
9. A submarine
10. Chicago

a) "Stella Dallas"
b) "The Goldbergs"
c) "Night Beat"
d) "Adventures of Nero Wolfe"
e) "The Mel Blanc Show"
f) "Hannibal Cobb"
g) "Red Hook-31"
h) "Seth Parker"
i) "The Musical Steelmakers"
j) "Latitude Zero"

115. Letting Bygones Be Bygones

Answer true or false:

1. There are no checkers in Chinese Checkers.

‎——————

2. An ex-President once swore in another President.

‎——————

3. James C. Petrillo headed the AF of L.

‎——————

4. Andy Hardy's father was played by Charles Coburn.

‎——————

5. Gloria Swanson's real name is Lucille LeSueur.

‎——————

6. Wild Bill Elliott's horse was named Duke.

‎——————

7. During World War II, Rosie was a railwayman.

‎——————

8. Nylon was withheld from civilian use because it was needed for parachutes in WW II.

‎——————

9. Lady Nancy Astor, the English Member of Parliament, was actually born in Virginia.

‎——————

10. Dorothy Parker was the first woman columnist to report the rise of Hitler.

116. Headline News

To what news events do these headlines refer?

1. FOREIGNER BECOMES HEAD OF OUR COUNTRY

---

2. "1600 PENNSY AVE." NEW RADIO HIT

---

3. 5—COUNT THEM—5

---

4. HAUPTMANN NAILED FOR KIDNAPING

---

5. PRESTER JOHN'S KINGDOM INVADED

---

6. "YOU CAN'T HAVE 15" SAYS SENATE TO FDR

---

7. BIGGEST SHOW ON EARTH OPENS AT FLUSHING MEADOW

---

8. EX-RED CHIEF SLAIN

9. IF YOUR PAY ENVELOPE'S LIGHTER, HERE'S WHY

10. NAZI COUNTERBLOW IN BELGIUM

117. Ten Great Oldies

Match the artists and their songs:

1.	Hazel Scott	a)	"South American Way"
2.	Dinah Shore	b)	"Marta"
3.	Vaughn Monroe	c)	"Ain't Misbehavin'"
4.	Shirley Temple	d)	"Franklin D. Roosevelt Jones"
5.	Arthur Tracy	e)	"Cabin in the Sky"
6.	Fats Waller	f)	"Shoofly Pie and Apple Pan Dowdy"
7.	Ethel Waters	g)	"Racing With the Moon"
8.	Bert Williams	h)	"On The Good Ship Lollipop"
9.	Carmen Miranda	i)	"Over the Rainbow"
10.	Judy Garland	j)	"Nobody"

153

118. Theme Songs

Match the theme and the band:

1. "Let's Dance"	a) Vincent Lopez
2. "Christopher Columbus"	b) Woody Herman
3. "Quaker City Jazz"	c) Hal Kemp
4. "Star Dreams"	d) Jan Savitt
5. "Blue Flame"	e) Benny Goodman
6. "Tuxedo Junction"	f) Glenn Miller
7. "Nola"	g) Charlie Spivak
8. "Swing Out"	h) Fletcher Henderson
9. "How I'll Miss You"	i) Erskine Hawkins
10. "Moonlight Serenade"	j) Chick Webb

119. Baseball Monickers

Identify the baseball player from his nickname:

1. High Pockets

_____

2. The Iron Horse

3. Goose

_____

4. Little Poison

_____

5. Three-Fingered

_____

6. Gabby

_____

7. Bucky

_____

8. Rube

_____

9. The Trojan

_____

10. Lippy

120. D. C. Relics

𝒟 𝒟 𝒟 𝒟 𝒟 𝒟

1. Who was Vice President in: a) 1929; b) 1933; c) 1941; d) 1945; e) 1949?

_____

2. Whose Vice President said, "What this country needs is a good 5¢ cigar"?

_____

3. What did all these men have in common: J. Howard McGrath, Tom C. Clark, Francis Biddle, Robert H. Jackson, and Frank Murphy?

_____

4. Who ran for Vice President on the Landon ticket in 1936?

_____

5. What Kansas senator also published farm magazines?

_____

6. Both these men had served in their youth in the naval ministries of their countries. In 1941, they met off the coast of Newfoundland, on two vessels. Who were they? What was the meeting about?

_____

7. This woman had four sons; all of them were in the service. One was a Marine captain; the second, an air corps captain; the last two, naval ensigns. What were their names and the name of their mother?

8. Harry Hopkins headed an organization in the 30s with a $550 million budget that paid its workers approximately $50 a month. What was it?

9. What New Deal cabinet posts did these people fill: a) Cordell Hull; b) James A. Farley; c) Harold L. Ickes; d) Henry Morgenthau?

10. What happened to J. P. Morgan when he attended the Senate Banking and Currency inquiry of 1933?

121. Movie Mnemonics

1. "Garbo talks!" In what film?

2. Who was the doggy hero of the Blondie series?

3. What was the role played by Claude Rains in *Here Comes Mr. Jordan*, Robert Cummings in *Heaven Only Knows*, and Cary Grant in *The Bishop's Wife*?

---

4. What ailment afflicted Ronald Colman in *Random Harvest*, John Hodiak in *Somewhere in the Night*, Joan Crawford in *Possessed*, Gregory Peck in *Mirage*, and Dan Duryea in *Black Angel*?

---

5. With which studio, revered by the avant-garde French director, Jean-Luc Godard, do you associate Frankie Darro, The East Side Kids, and the Bowery Boys?

---

6. Name the film in which Charles Boyer did *not* say, "Come with me to the Casbah!"

---

7. What was the name of the German shepherd who was first a war hero, later a movie star?

---

8. Hedwig Eva Maria Kiesler Mandl Markey is the real name of what movie star?

---

9. "Gable's back and Garson's got him!" In what film?

---

10. Richard Conte is to Dane Clark as James Whitmore is to _____ _____?

122. Radio Locales

Match the radio show with its location:

1. The Jot'em Down Store, Pine Ridge, Arkansas
2. 79 Wistful Vista
3. Just off Hollywood Blvd., and one flight up
4. The Crystal Studio
5. Rushville Center
6. Black Swan Hall
7. The Capitol Theatre, N.Y.C.
8. The Little Theatre off Times Square
9. The town of Preston
10. Sandy Harbor

a) "The Roxy Gang"

b) "Ethel and Albert"
c) "Lum 'n' Abner"

d) "First Nighter"
e) "Fibber McGee and Molly"
f) "Joyce Jordan, M.D."
g) "I Love a Mystery"

h) "Our Gal Sunday"

i) "Make Believe Ballroom"
j) "Ma Perkins"

123. Live from Hollywood

1. *Time* Magazine called this "easily the greatest war picture." It was written by Laurence Stallings, directed by King Vidor, and it starred John Gilbert and Renee Adoree. What was its name?

---

2. What was Spangler Arlington Brugh's nom de cinema?

---

3. Two movies having nothing in common shared the same name. One was directed by De Mille and featured flashbacks all the way back to the Bible; the other featured Tracy and Hepburn as married—and opposing—lawyers. What was the name of both films?

---

4. What was the name of the Bogart character in *Petrified Forest*?

---

5. Tarzan in the movies has been played by fourteen actors. How many can you name?

---

6. Who portrayed these painters in the movies: a) Rembrandt; b) Gaugin; c) Toulouse-Lautrec; d) Van Gogh; e) Michelangelo?

---

7. Who directed *Nanook of the North, Man of Aran, Louisiana Story*, etc.?

---

8. Who played: a) The Tin Woodman; b) The Scarecrow; c) The Cowardly Lion; d) The Wicked Witch; e) The Wizard?

---

9. Who starred in the first 3-D movie?

---

10. Who played "The Thing"?

124. For the Duration

1. What did these acronyms stand for: a) WAACS; b) WAVES; c) WAFS; d) SPARS?

---

2. What organization fixed price ceilings on all commodities and controlled rents in defense areas?

---

3. What did all these have in common: auto tires, sugar, coffee, gasoline, fuel oil, meat, fats and oils, butter, cheese, processed foods, and shoes?

---

4. He retired first as a four-star general, then was called back into the army, but as a three-star general—and was later promoted to five-star general. His name?

---

5. A department store executive in 1941, reporting on a riot, said, "When the doors opened at 9:30, they fell flat on their faces." Why the riot?

---

6. Whose facilities were taken over on December 28, 1944?

---

7. What did these men have in common: George Sylvester Viereck, William Dudley Pelley, and Gerald Winrod?

8. What was H. R. Bill No. 1776: a) GI Bill of Rights; b) The Lend-Lease Bill; c) Emergency Price Control Act?

9. What was the claim to fame of Congresswoman Jeanette Rankin?

10. It was ugly, stubby, skittery. It could double in brass as a troop carrier, weapons carrier, or communications truck, and it could pull light field pieces. It was named after a character in "Popeye ('Thimble Theater')." What was it?

125. What's on Tonight?

1. "America's . . ." was the first word in the title of these three shows. Can you identify them? a) This show featured Orson Welles and Joseph Cotten; b) this one adapted such plays as *A Trip to Chinatown*; and c) this was a discussion program.

2. At one time called "Watch the Fords Go By," this comedy show featured Elmer Blurt, a painfully shy door-to-door salesman, and Tizzie Lish. What was its name?

_____

3. Singing groups on what variety show included the Mariners, the Chordettes, and the Jubalaires?

_____

4. Two "Amazing Mr. . . ." shows had well-known actors playing the leads. Can you name them, and their shows?

_____

5. Walter Winchell once won $500 on this show, which gave away Pall Mall Awards of Merit. What was its name?

_____

6. Who was "friend of those who need a friend; enemy to those who make him an enemy"?

_____

7. Pam always shrieked, "Look out, Jerry! He's got a gun!" Who were Pam and Jerry?

_____

8. Before becoming a top TV producer, Sheldon Leonard was one of the busiest and best radio actors around. One of his characters, Orville Sharp, used to ask, "Am I corr-ek-itt?" On what show?

_____

9. Who used to intone, "Invoke legem magiciacorum"?

_____

10. Who always took the same train every week at the same time?

126. Old Clothes

~~~~~~

1. What had a reet pleat, a rough cuff, and peg pants?

_____

2. What was a claw-hammer?

_____

3. What was a fore-and-aft hat?

_____

4. What kind of hat did Happy Hooligan wear?

_____

5. What was a "dickey"?

_____

6. What was a "gertrude"?

_____

7. Who gave her name to the "alice blue gown"?

_____

8. What was a skimmer?

_____

9. Wilson wore pince nez. What were they?

_____

10. Doughboys and Boy Scouts once wore puttees. What were they?

127. Dating Game

🍂 🍂 🍂 🍂 🍂 🍂

Match the old-fashioned item in Column I with its modern-day equivalent in column II:

I	II
1. Frigidaire	a) nightstick
2. Victrola	b) dentures
3. Tidy	c) refrigerator
4. Velocipede	d) doily
5. Plus-fours	e) wristwatch
6. Billy	f) record player
7. Four-in-hand	g) trousers
8. Hunter	h) tie
9. Drummer	i) bicycle
10. Choppers	j) salesman

128. By Their Hits Ye Shall Know Them

◌ ◌ ◌ ◌ ◌ ◌

What songs do you associate with these recording stars?

1. Johnnie Ray
2. Blue Barron
3. Eileen Barton
4. Teresa Brewer
5. Perry Como
6. Bing Crosby
7. Bing Crosby and the Andrews Sisters
8. Doris Day

9. Jimmy Dorsey
10. Tommy Dorsey
11. Vaughn Monroe
12. Russ Morgan
13. Patti Page
14. Les Paul and Mary Ford
15. Lanny Ross

a) "Sunday, Monday or Always"
b) "Ballerina"
c) "Amapola"
d) "Cry"
e) "Pistol Packin' Mama"
f) "Prisoner of Love"
g) "Cruisin' Down the River"

h) "If I Knew You Were Comin' I'd've Baked a Cake"
i) "How High the Moon"
j) "Cruisin' Down The River"
k) "Stay As Sweet As You Are"
l) "I'll Never Smile Again"
m) "It's Magic"
n) "Music, Music, Music"
o) "Mockin'bird Hill"

129. Nicknames

1. Who is the Lion of Judah?

_____

2. Identify "The Tombs."

_____

3. Who was the "Flying Finn"?

_____

4. Who was the "man of a thousand faces"?

_____

5. Who was "Little Poker Face"?

_____

6. Who was the football coach known as "Gloomy Gil"?

_____

7. Who was the "Bishop of Broadway"?

_____

8. Who was "The March King"?

_____

9. Who was "The Bambino"?

_____

10. What was a "dollar-a-year man"?

130. Organizations

1. What was the "invisible empire"?

_____

2. Who said, "A man may be down but he's never out"?

_____

3. What organization was headed by Dan Beard?

_____

4. Identify the fraternal order: a) IOOF; b) FOE; c) WOW; d) K of P; e) K of C; f) BPOE.

_____

5. Whose motto is "Service"?

_____

6. Who initiated the "Moral Rearmament" program to bring about world peace?

_____

7. Who were the ABC powers?

_____

8. What were the Wobblies?

_____

9. What was the Hays Office?

_____

10. What was the WCTU?

131. Box Office

𝒯 𝒯 𝒯 𝒯 𝒯 𝒯 𝒯

1. What do Edmund Gwenn, Bob Hope, and Monty Woolley have in common?

_____

2. William Powell played Philo Vance in Paramount's *Canary Murder Case*. Who was Philo Vance in MGM's *Bishop Murder Case*?

_____

3. How did Lon Chaney betray his real identity while on the witness stand in *The Unholy Three*?

_____

4. Who was: a) The Body; b) The Look; c) The Legs?

_____

5. Joan Fontaine is to Olivia de Havilland as June Havoc is to _____?

_____

6. What was the earnest warning at the end of *Dracula*?

_____

7. Who led two lives as a movie producer (*Carnegie Hall*) and as a real-life counterspy?

_____

8. Who played Boston Blackie?

9. In what picture did Marlene Dietrich stride into the Sahara in high heels to follow her lover?

10. What was Earl Derr Biggers's most famous creation?

132. Dialing the Job

What was the profession or occupation of each of the following mythical radio characters?

1. David Harding   a) Detective
2. Don Winslow   b) Aviator
3. Steve Adams   c) Wealthy young man about town
4. Steve Wilson   d) Rancher & Straight Arrow
5. Richard Diamond   e) Counterspy
6. Rocky King   f) Insurance investigator
7. Hop Harrigan   g) Private detective
8. Lorenzo Jones   h) Naval commander
9. Lamont Cranston   i) Mechanic
10. Johnny Dollar   j) Newspaper editor

133. Music Makers

Match the movie musical biography with the subject:

1. Sol Hurok	a) *Words and Music*
2. George M. Cohan	b) *Three Little Words*
3. Sigmund Romberg	c) *Night and Day*
4. Johann Strauss	d) *Tonight We Sing*
5. Jane Froman	e) *Yankee Doodle Dandy*
6. Frédéric Chopin	f) *I'll See You in My Dreams*
7. Lillian Roth	g) *The Great Waltz*
8. Ruth Etting	h) *So This is Love*
9. Gertrude Lawrence	i) *Till The Clouds Roll By*
10. Fanny Brice	j) *A Song to Remember*
11. Grace Moore	k) *With A Song in My Heart*
12. Rodgers and Hart	l) *I'll Cry Tomorrow*
13. Jerome Kern	m) *Star*
14. Gus Kahn	n) *Funny Girl*
15. Bert Kalmar and Harry Ruby	o) *Love Me or Leave Me*
16. Cole Porter	p) *Deep in My Heart*

134. Sobriquets

1. Who were "The Sons of The Wild Jackass"?

_____

2. What was "The Lost Battalion"?

_____

3. Who was "The Swedish Match King"?

_____

4. What was The Bank Holiday?

_____

5. What was the Brain Trust?

_____

6. What was a doubledecker?

_____

7. What was "We Do Our Part"?

_____

8. What was the good neighbor policy?

_____

9. Who was the old curmudgeon?

_____

10. What was "Thought Control"?

135. Strange Names

1. On Leongs and Hip Sings were: a) Chinese dishes which were Americanized into chop suey and egg foo yung; b) rival fighting tongs; c) first-generation and second-generation Chinese-Americans?

2. Moresnet was: a) a neutralized country at the intersection of Holland, Belgium, and Germany; b) the first home permanent; c) head of a French terrorist group during the 30s.

3. Why did Pullman cars have such elaborate names? a) They were subsidized by the communities thus honored; b) to help passengers remember their cars; c) George Pullman's first job was that of a map maker.

4. Define a) snowbird; b) dick; c) harness bull; d) dip; e) roscoe.

5. Who were "The Big Four?"

6. Who was "The Big Six"?

7. Who were "The Big Three"?

8. What were "white wings"?

9. Who was "Cactus Jack"?

10. Who invented the term, "Veep"?

136. Movie Bands

Match the bands with the movie in which they appeared:

1. *Best Foot Forward*   a) Kay Kyser
2. *Hollywood Hotel*   b) Jimmy Dorsey
3. *Dancing Co-Ed*   c) Harry James
4. *The Fleet's In*   d) Glenn Miller
5. *Winter Wonderland*   e) Benny Goodman
6. *Las Vegas Nights*   f) Woody Herman
7. *Swing Fever*   g) Tommy Dorsey
8. *Orchestra Wives*   h) Artie Shaw

137. Just Good Friends

1. Who was Little Orphan Annie's boyfriend?

   _____

2. Who was Britt Reid's secretary?

   _____

3. Who was Kathleen Anderson?

4. Who was the society editor on Steve Wilson's *Illustrated Press*?

5. Who was Leila Ransom?

6. Kitty Archer was whose mouse?

7. Della Street took dictation from whom?

8. Who was Lamont Cranston's friend and companion?

9. Irene Adler was the only woman to which detective?

10. Ann Williams and a certain staffer on *The Morning Express* had something going. What was his name?

138. Stable Mates

We've corralled the steeds of some popular heroes. Can you sort them out and give each rider his own horse?

Victor, Diablo, Silver, Tarzan, Buttermilk, Champion, Tony, Rex, Scout, Trigger

a) Cisco Kid _____
b) Tonto _____
c) Roy Rogers _____
d) Tom Mix _____
e) Dale Evans _____
f) Ken Maynard _____
g) Sgt. Preston _____
h) Dan Reed _____
i) The Lone Ranger _____
j) Gene Autry _____

139. Mixed Drinks

1. If you mixed two ice cubes, ½ lime, 1 jigger of rum, and Coca-Cola, what would you get?

___

2. What cocktail called for ⅓ Dry Gin, ⅓ French Vermouth, ⅓ Italian Vermouth, Dash of Orange Juice—shake with ice and strain into glass?

___

3. What two nonalcoholic substances when mixed together were supposed to get you drunk?

___

4. You had it if you were courageous; you could also drink it. What was it?

___

5. "Near beer" contained less than: a) 0.5 per cent alcohol; b) 2.5 per cent alcohol; c) 3.2 per cent alcohol; d) 4.4 per cent alcohol.

___

6. What were you served if you ordered any of these: angel foam, dry, fizz, giggle soup, Minnehaha, or sparkle?

___

7. What is: a) Coke-high; b) hardboiled lemonade; c) one-up; d) stinger?

___

8. What was the Rum Fleet?

___

9. Who were Izzie and Moe?

___

10. Who was Bishop Cannon?

140. Bank Night

✥ ✥ ✥ ✥ ✥ ✥

1. Norman Lloyd fell from the Statue of Liberty in what Hitchcock film?

_____

2. What was Jackie Jenkins's nickname?

_____

3. Who was a fugitive from a chain gang?

_____

4. The quickly aging refugee from Shangri La was played by Maria Marguerita Guadelupe Boldao y Castilla. What was her name in the movies?

_____

5. Who used to blurt out, "Woo-woo!"? (*Hellzapoppin'* and *Cracked Nuts*)

_____

6. Harlow changed into "something more comfortable" for Ben Lyon in what movie?

_____

7. What do all these songs have in common: "We're in the Money," "I've Got to Sing a Torch Song," "Remember My Forgotten Man," "Petting in The Park," and "Shadow Waltz"?

_____

8. What is the film capital's theme song, and who first sang it in what movie?

9. Who played the junior Nazi in *Tomorrow the World*?

10. Fred and Ginger were the second bananas in *Flying Down to Rio*. Who were the actual headliners?

141. They Don't Build 'Em That Way Anymore

1. The capacity of Radio City Music Hall is: a) 1,500; b) 2,500; c) 4,000; d) 6,200.

2. How high is the Empire State Building?

3. Prior to 1930, what was the tallest building in the world?

---

4. What famous hotel was formerly on the site of the Empire State Building?

---

5. What is "Kodak City"?

---

6. What were Hoovervilles?

---

7. Who sculpted the faces on Mt. Rushmore?

---

8. His companies helped build the Grand Coulee Dam, the San Francisco–Oakland Bridge, cargo ships, freighters, and destroyers. Who was he?

---

9. What is the "Flatiron"?

---

10. Who designed the Imperial Hotel, Tokyo?

142. An All-time Swing Band

The boys have got a gig tonight, but unless somebody straightens out the instruments, nobody's going to make any music. Can you assign the correct instrument to each player?

cornet, vibes, trombone, bass, alto sax, tenor sax, guitar, baritone sax, clarinet, piano

    a)   Bix Beiderbecke _____
    b)   Jack Teagarden _____
    c)   Charlie Parker _____
    d)   Stan Getz _____
    e)   Gerry Mulligan _____
    f)   Peewee Russell _____
    g)   Art Tatum _____
    h)   Charlie Christian _____
    i)   John Kirby _____
    j)   Lionel Hampton _____

143. Music Notes

1. Davey Tough and Buddy Rich had what in common?

2. Who sang "720 in the Books" with the Jan Savitt band?

---

3. Who sang "Deep Purple" for Larry Clinton?

---

4. Which record company owned the Bluebird label?

---

5. Cecil Mack and Jimmy Johnston introduced this dance in 1923. What was it?

---

6. What was Benny Goodman's first radio show?

---

7. What was the name of a Benny Goodman television special?

---

8. Who was "Her Nibs"?

---

9. Who was "The Poet of the Violin"?

---

10. "Six Lessons from Madame La Zonga" was this vocalist's best-selling record for 1940. What was her name?

144. And Now a Word from...

Do you remember who sponsored these radio shows?

1. "The Right to Happiness"
2. "Ma Perkins"
3. "Little Orphan Annie"
4. "Manhattan Merry Go Round"
5. "Metropolitan Opera"
6. "Quick as a Flash"
7. "Dr. I.Q."
8. "Edgar Bergen and Charlie McCarthy Show"
9. "The Jack Benny Show"
10. "Screen Guild Theatre"

a) Mars Candy Co.
b) Gulf
c) Ivory Soap
d) Chase and Sanborn
e) Oxydol
f) Jell-O
g) Ovaltine
h) Helbros Watches
i) Texaco
j) Dr. Lyon's Tooth Powder

145. Inventors

1. Major Edwin H. Armstrong broadcast from Radio Station W1XOJ, Worcester, Mass., to demonstrate what invention?

_____

2. What do these inventors have in common: Lewis, Maxim, Browning, and Vickers?

_____

3. Why is Dr. J. S. Pemberton remembered so fondly in Atlanta, Ga.?

_____

4. What invention was Robert H. Goddard largely responsible for?

_____

5. In 1932, Edwin H. Land invented a new kind of glass. What was it?

_____

6. Who invented the blendor?

_____

7. Who was responsible for the Shasta daisy, the white blackberry, and the plumcot?

_____

8. What did Charles Kettering invent?

_____

9. Who invented "The Magic Bullet" (*606*)?

_____

10. What wartime device did Sir Douglas Watson Watts invent?

146. Rummaging Through the Attic

Check the word or phrase closest in nostalgic meaning to the key word:

1. *Spats*—a) fights; b) a baby fish; c) shoe protector; d) love taps

_____

2. *Knickerbockers*—a) New York ball team; b) Dutchmen; c) trousers; d) beer steins

_____

3. *Templar*—a) author; b) Freemason; c) hat; d) church architect

_____

4. *Alky-cooking*—a) outdoor barbecue; b) illicit distilling; c) bartending; d) cheap gas range

_____

5. *Bunion Derby*—a) marathon race; b) podiatry school; c) breadline; d) man's hat

_____

6. *Curb market*—a) outdoor bazaar; b) stock exchange; c) street building monopoly; d) artificial business slowdown

7. *Bobbing*—a) Hallowe'en sport; b) hair treatment; c) draft-dodging; d) vote buying

8. *R–34*—a) transatlantic dirigible; b) Republican convention ballot that nominated Harding; c) variety of influenza; d) cipher used in the Zimmerman Telegram

9. *Interurban*—a) streetcar line; b) county form of government; c) suburban; d) pseudo-sophisticated

10. *Middletown*—a) sociological survey; b) city residential district; c) top movie of 1930; d) Coolidge's hometown

11. *Ponzi Plan*—a) get-rich-quick scheme; b) Italian disarmament policy; c) health-through-dancing fad; d) tomato-based cuisine

12. *Grimes Reflex*—a) medical syndrome; b) radio circuit; c) economic reaction; d) bridge bid

13. *Hall–Mills*—a) vaudeville team; b) murder case; c) investment trust; d) hotel chain

14. *Cloche*—a) woman's hat; b) French dance; c) Swiss chronometer; d) cocktail

15. *Plumb Plan*—a) railroad management scheme; b) water-supply innovation; c) California agriculture board; d) Virgin Islands government plan

147. Remotes, Pickups, and Transcriptions

1. How many Mountie radio shows do you remember?

_____

2. Terry was "the second Mrs. Burton." Who was the first?

_____

3. Whose band did contestants lead in "So You Want to Lead a Band?"

_____

4. Complete this: Commissioner Gordon was to Batman as _____ was to the Shadow.

_____

5. Romance can live on at 35—so proved the heroine of which soap opera?

_____

6. Dr. Brent was to call surgery at the beginning of which soap opera?

_____

7. What story reflected the courage, spirit, and integrity of American women everywhere?

_____

8. What instrument did Evelyn play in Phil Spitalny's All-Girl Orchestra?

9. On this detective show Jack Webb was the hero; Raymond Burr, the Inspector. What was its name?

10. What did you have to send in if you wanted a Little Orphan Annie Shake-up Mug?

148. Western Memories

1. How many Clark Gable westerns can you remember?

2. "The Trampas Walk" is Hollywood's term for the classic confrontation of good guy and bad guy on the main street of a cow town. Who was Trampas?

3. How many Ray Milland westerns can you remember?

4. How many Frank Sinatra westerns can you remember?

5. How many Humphrey Bogart westerns can you name?

6. How many of the sidekicks who rode with Hopalong Cassidy do you remember?

———

7. How many James Cagney westerns can you name?

———

8. Who played Cochise in *Broken Arrow*?

———

9. How many Cisco Kids can you name?

———

10. How many Joan Crawford westerns can you name?

149. Kilocycle Queries

1. What was Harry Frankel's radio name?

———

2. What tender, human story of young married love was dedicated to everyone who has ever been in love?

———

3. Pat Ryan and Flip Corkin appeared on what show?

4. Who was the emcee of "Truth or Consequences"?

5. Who were "Mr. Hush," "Miss Hush," and "The Walking Man"?

6. What was the original name of "The $64 Question"?

7. Why were certain tales able to keep you in . . . "Suspense"?

8. The Heart Line was a feature of what show?

9. Who saw her own beloved daughter, Laurel, marry into wealth and society, and, realizing the differences in their tastes and worlds, went out of Laurel's life?

10. Who was "The Silver-Masked Tenor"?

150. Royalty

1. King Haakon VII ruled what country?

_____

2. What World War I ruler had a withered arm?

_____

3. What popular king died in a mountain-climbing accident?

_____

4. Irving Berlin dedicated what song to what queen when she visited America?

_____

5. President Roosevelt fed which royal guests on hot dogs when they visited him?

_____

6. Who was the Kaiser-in-Hind?

_____

7. Who "suspended the exercise of royal power" and went into exile, April 1931: a) King Zog of Albania; b) King Alfonso of Spain; c) King Humbert of Italy; d) King Peter of Yugoslavia?

_____

8. Was Edward VIII the first king of the House of Windsor?

_____

9. What movie starred Bruce Cabot, Fay Wray, and an island dweller who couldn't stand Spads?

_____

10. Which band leader was known as the Waltz King?

Answers

1. *Foreign Correspondent*
2. *Above Suspicion*
3. *Dragon Seed*
4. *Since You Went Away*
5. *Casablanca*
6. *The Woman in White*
7. *Citizen Kane*
8. *Man Hunt*
9. *The Man Who Came To Dinner*
10. *Night Must Fall*

2.

1. Kryptonite
2. Anything yellow
3. Skeezix Wallett
4. In the center of the Earth
5. "The Brownies"
6. John Tinney McCutcheon
7. Ignatz Mouse
8. He was a fireman
9. By the yellow and black striped belt
10. Bucky, Toro, Tubby, Knuckles, Jefferson Worthington Sandervilt, and Whitewash Jones

3.

1. George Santayana
2. *See Here, Private Hargrove*
3. Andrew Carnegie and Dale Carnegie
4. Maurice Chevalier
5. Leslie Howard
6. Robert Young
7. mehitabel
8. The line of the 1936-37 Fordham football team
9. Oscar
10. Ezio Pinza

4.

1-h, 2-g, 3-i, 4-f, 5-j, 6-e, 7-k, 8-d, 9-l, 10-c, 11-m, 12-b, 13-n, 14-o, 15-a

5.

1. Campana's Italian Balm
2. Mennen's Shaving Cream
3. The Savage Automatic Pistol
4. Prince Albert and Tuxedo
5. —and Almond Cream"
6. Sloan's (a liniment; the others are toothpastes)
7. a
8. General Motors
9. Borden's
10. Wurlitzer

6.

1. Jeanne Eagels
2. *The Emperor Jones*
3. George Bernard Shaw; it was originally *Arms And The Man*
4. Fred Astaire
5. First play to run more than 1,000 performances
6. *The Hot Mikado* and *The Swing Mikado*
7. *The Little Show*
8. *As Thousands Cheer*
9. Anne Nichols
10. Fannie Brice and Billy Rose

7.

1. They were all fictional detectives
2. Characters in *The Grapes of Wrath*; later, by extension, all migratory workers
3. Popular illustrators, especially of children's books
4. a) James Whitcomb Riley; b) Don Marquis; c) Gelett Burgess
5. Carl Sandburg
6. a) writer of dog stories; b) long distance walker
7. a) Edna St. Vincent Millay; b) Kathleen Millay; c) Norma Millay
8. Theodore Dreiser, brother of Paul Dresser
9. They were all dress designers
10. Thomas Wolfe

8.

1-h, 2-i, 3-m, 4-n, 5-l, 6-o, 7-j, 8-k, 9-a, 10-g, 11-b, 12-f, 13-c, 14-e, 15-d

9.

1. "Someday I'll Find You," by Noel Coward.
2. "Les Preludes" by Liszt and "Fingal's Cave" by Mendelssohn
3. "Lorenzo Jones"
4. "Burns and Allen"
5. "Uncle Don"
6. "The Happiness Boys"
7. "Just Plain Bill"
8. Little Orphan Annie
9. "Love in Bloom"
10. "Terry and the Pirates"

10.

1. Schoolboy stories
2. They were all playwrights
3. William Allen White
4. *The Nation*
5. Dog stories
6. P. G. Wodehouse
7. Upton Sinclair; "Lanny Budd"
8. Paddy Chayevsky
9. William Saroyan
10. Joseph E. Davies

11.

1-o, 2-g, 3-n, 4-f, 5-m, 6-e, 7-l, 8-d, 9-k, 10-c, 11-j, 12-b, 13-i, 14-a, 15-h

12.

    1. Elizabeth Arden
    2. Spinach
    3. "Happy Days Are Here Again"
    4. Sing Sing
    5. Eleanor Roosevelt
    6. The assassin of Huey Long
    7. The Lincoln penny
    8. The YMCA
    9. Russian secret police
   10. Uncle Bim from Australia

13.

1-d, 2-g, 3-f, 4-c, 5-j, 6-h, 7-i, 8-b, 9-e, 10-a

14.

1-g, 2-i, 3-j, 4-l, 5-n, 6-o, 7-m, 8-k, 9-c, 10-b, 11-a, 12-d, 13-e, 14-f, 15-h

15.

    1. *Liberty*
    2. *Judge*
    3. *The New Yorker*; Harold Ross
    4. *The Literary Digest*
    5. Bernarr Macfadden
    6. *The Police Gazette*
    7. *Vanity Fair*
    8. *Smart Set*
    9. *Time*
   10. *The Saturday Evening Post*

16.

1. It had triple ignition and 18 spark plugs
2. The 1917 Ford; it sold for $360.00
3. It was the first aircraft carrier, 1922
4. No difference
5. The *Winnie Mae*
6. The sleeve valve
7. Lt. Commander Richard E. Byrd
8. Planetary
9. The Hudson River
10. Labrador, Canada

17.

1. A racing car driver
2. He was Warren Harding's Airedale
3. Jess Willard
4. Horse racing—they were all jockeys
5. Prize fighting
6. Swimming
7. The pole vault
8. Pocket billiards
9. They were all long distance runners
10. Professional wrestling

18.

1-f, 2-h, 3-g, 4-j, 5-i, 6-c, 7-d, 8-b, 9-a, 10-e

19.

1. Time, bulb, instantaneous
2. The Packard
3. Happiness Candy Stores
4. Ipana toothpaste
5. KDKA (Pittsburgh, Pa.)
6. Listerine

7. Trinity College, Durham, N.C., changed its name to Duke University
8. Davison
9. Not the baseball player. It was named for the daughter of President Grover Cleveland, Baby Ruth.
10. b

20.

1-f, 2-e, 3-h, 4-j, 5-m, 6-o, 7-a, 8-b, 9-c, 10-i, 11-l, 12-d, 13-k, 14-n, 15-g

21.

1. a)   to prosecute to the limit of the law
   b)   perpetrated within this county
   c)   the rights and privileges of all its citizens
2. a)   a cloud of dust and a hearty hi-yo, Silver!
   b)   daring and resourceful
   c)   fight for law and order
   d)   find a greater champion of justice
   e)   those thrilling days of yesteryear
   f)   thundering hoofbeats of the great horse, Silver
3. a)   Show them how we stand!
   b)   Have you tried Wheaties?
   c)   Won't you try Wheaties?
   d)   And neither will you.
   e)   So just buy Wheaties,
4. a)   many things, for I walk by night
   b)   hidden in the hearts of men and women who have stepped into the shadows
   c)   nameless terrors

22.

1-c, 2-h, 3-e, 4-g, 5-a, 6-i, 7-d, 8-j, 9-f, 10-b

23.

1-c, 2-l, 3-k, 4-i, 5-j, 6-h, 7-g, 8-e, 9-d, 10-f, 11-b, 12-a

24.

1. Ernie Pyle
2. a) *The Morro Castle*; b) *The Normandie*
3. Tommy Dorsey
4. Thomas B. Costain
5. a) Walter Pitkin; b) Joshua Liebman; c) Fulton J. Sheen
6. Antarctica
7. a) Berlin; b) New York City; c) Cairo; d) Saratoga Springs
8. He developed Argyrol
9. The four chaplains who gave up their life jackets to others and went down with a sinking troopship
10. A showboat; *Cotton Blossom*

25.

1. Pola Negri
2. *Our Town*
3. *Cimarron*
4. a) Deanna Durbin; b) Freddie Bartholemew; c) Jackie Coogan; d) Elizabeth Taylor; e) Shirley Temple
5. *Wuthering Heights*
6. Mary Astor
7. a) Lew Ayers; b) Jean Hersholt; c) Lionel Barrymore
8. *Key Largo*
9. *Road to Singapore*, 1940
10. Gary Cooper; *Morocco*

26.

1. Al Smith
2. Don Marquis
3. Carl Sandburg
4. Ethel Barrymore
5. W. C. Fields
6. Will Rogers
7. Douglas MacArthur
8. Grantland Rice
9. Edgar Guest
10. Texas Guinan

27.

1-h, 2-d, 3-i, 4-c, 5-j, 6-g, 7-b, 8-f, 9-a, 10-e

28.

1-c, 2-j, 3-e, 4-f, 5-g, 6-h, 7-i, 8-b, 9-a, 10-d

29.

1-d, 2-e, 3-a, 4-g, 5-b, 6-h, 7-c, 8-i, 9-j, 10-f

30.

1. a) Renfield; b) Col. Moran
2. The drug that kept The Mummy going
3. Jack Benny
4. King Kong
5. *The Blue Bird*
6. They all played the Devil
7. They all played Dr. Jekyll
8. Peter Lorre in *M*
9. Lionel Atwill
10. Charles Laughton was Dr. Moreau; Bela Lugosi was The Sayer of the Law

31.

1. Jimmie Durante and Eddie Jackson
2. Will Rogers; W. C. Fields; Fred Allen (also W. C. Fields)
3. Sir Harry Lauder
4. a) *What Price Glory*; b) *Life With Father*; c) *Victoria Regina*; d) *Strange Interlude*
5. A vaudeville tramp cyclist
6. They were all vaudeville circuits
7. Vernon Castle
8. Joe Penner
9. Joe Cook
10. Flo Ziegfeld

32.

1. a) Elizabeth; b) Mohandas; c) Vladimir (sometimes Nikolai); d) Benito
2. Blue Boy
3. Al Smith
4. It was a double play executed by ball players Joe Tinker, Johnny Evers, and Frank Chance when they played shortstop, second, and first base on the Chicago Cubs
5. "Keeping Up With the Jones's"
6. Dr. Wilhelm Reich
7. Number One Checkerboard Square, St. Louis, Missouri
8. T–M Bar Ranch, Dobie Township
9. Dr. Emile Coué
10. Wendell Willkie

33.

1-e, 2-c, 3-g, 4-j, 5-b, 6-i, 7-h, 8-f, 9-a, 10-d

34.

1. a) Damon Runyon; b) Ring Lardner; c) Paul Gallico; d) Westbrook Pegler
2. Zane Grey
3. "The Rover Boys"
4. Louis Bromfield
5. Booth Tarkington
6. a) Hervey Allen; b) Kenneth Roberts; c) Joseph Hergesheimer; d) Charles Nordhoff and James Norman Hall
7. James Branch Cabell
8. George
9. Clare Boothe Luce
10. Ben Hecht

35.

1-d, 2-j, 3-e, 4-i, 5-f, 6-c, 7-h, 8-b, 9-g, 10-a

36.

1. Wally Cox, Tony Randall, Marion Lorne, Patricia Benoit
2. Leon Ames
3. Kuda Bux
4. They were some of the stars on Ed Sullivan's first "Toast of the Town" show (June 20, 1948)
5. Ben Alexander
6. Ernie Kovacs
7. Roger Price
8. Red Buttons
9. Marguerite Piazza, the Hamilton Trio, The Billy Williams Quartet, and Bambi Linn and Rod Alexander
10. Jackie Gleason

37.

1. ". . . break your back."
2. ". . . to know one."
3. ". . . losers weepers."
4. ". . . you're glue."
5. ". . . a bottle of ink."

38.

1. The Big Parade
2. Command Decision
3. The Bridges At Toko-Ri
4. Hell's Angels
5. Guadalcanal Diary
6. I Wanted Wings
7. The Bridge On The River Kwai
8. The Story of G.I. Joe
9. Battleground
10. In Harm's Way

39.

1. Pluto
2. All science fiction magazines
3. a) Arthur Godfrey; b) Wendell Hall; c) Arthur Tracy; d) Jan Garber
4. a) Mischa Elman; b) Jascha Heifetz; c) Toscha Seidel
5. A strong man
6. Red Grange
7. A deer
8. Sir Cedric Hardwicke
9. Joseph Schildkraut
10. Max Liebman

40.

1-b, 2-d, 3-e, 4-g, 5-f, 6-c, 7-a

41.

1. Danny O'Day
2. Pinky Lee
3. Jerry Lester
4. Kathryn Murray
5. Dayton Allen, Bill Dana, Gabe Dell, Louis Nye, Don Knotts, Pat Harrington, Jr., Tom Poston
6. Art Baker
7. An announcer on "Toast of the Town"
8. Arthur Godfrey fired singer Julius La Rosa
9. The Continental
10. a) Sid Stone; b) George Gobel; c) Andy Devine

42.

1. Joe DiMaggio
2. Luis Firpo
3. Christy Mathewson
4. James J. Braddock
5. Norway. Pat O'Brien
6. Jack Dempsey
7. Yankee Stadium
8. Fielding H. Yost, University of Michigan
9. Lou Nova
10. Auto racing

43.

1. a) Pearl Buck; b) Winston Churchill (the American novelist); c) Ernest Hemingway; d) Jack London
2. *Ferdinand*—bull; *Bambi*—fawn; *Stuart Little*—mouse; *Babar*—elephant
3. a) Maine; b) Quebec; c) South Seas; d) Tibet; e) Czarist Russia
4. *The Green Hat*, under the nom de plume, Michael Arlen
5. Peter Bernard Kyne
6. Kathleen Norris
7. Charles Williams Eliot, president of Harvard, edited *The Harvard Classics* ("Dr. Eliot's Five-Foot Shelf")
8. Arthur Train
9. Sinclair Lewis
10. The English Roman Catholic writers, Hilaire Belloc and G. K. Chesterton

44.

1. "Information Please"
2. In *Three Little Pigs*
3. The USSR consulate
4. They were all concert pianists
5. Fr. Bernard Hubbard, S.J.
6. b
7. Buster Brown
8. Governor of Massachusetts
9. Postal Telegraph; Irving Berlin
10. A five-cent piece; in some locales, a cruising cab

45.

1-e, 2-g, 3-j, 4-a, 5-i, 6-d, 7-h, 8-b, 9-f, 10-c

46.

1. Lois Lane
2. Susan Kent
3. Sheena
4. Olive Oyl
5. Betty was the blonde, Veronica was the brunette
6. Sluggo dated Nancy, and Tubby dated Little Lulu
7. Miss Mizzou, Summer Smith Olson, Herself Muldoon, and Princess Snowflower
8. Mandrake's girl was Narda; Taia held hands with Ibis
9. Ellen Dolan
10. Minnie Ha-Cha

47.

1. Edna Ferber
2. Mazo de la Roche
3. Kathleen Norris
4. Elinor Glyn
5. Edna St. Vincent Millay
6. Margaret Sidney
7. Ella Wheeler Wilcox
8. Mary Roberts Rinehart
9. Margaretta Wade Campbell Deland
10. Ruth McKenney

48.

1. Mrs. Wallis Warfield Simpson
2. The same middle name—Spencer
3. Harry Hopkins
4. Franklin Delano Roosevelt
5. His father
6. Herbert Hoover
7. H. C. Wallace served under Coolidge; Henry Wallace under FDR
8. Mayor William Hale Thompson of Chicago
9. The American Legion
10. A Jersey City arena where Dempsey knocked out Carpentier in 1921

49.

1-e, 2-g, 3-i, 4-c, 5-k, 6-m, 7-o, 8-n, 9-l, 10-b, 11-j, 12-h, 13-f, 14-d, 15-a

50.

1. The B–26
2. The parachute
3. Glenn H. Curtiss
4. An English bomber
5. The autogiro
6. Three days, 19 hours, 8 minutes
7. Wiley Post, July 1933
8. The *Graf Zeppelin,* October 1928
9. General Italo Balbo
10. a

51.

1-c, 2-e, 3-h, 4-g, 5-j, 6-a, 7-i, 8-f, 9-b, 10-d

52.

1-g, 2-e, 3-c, 4-i, 5-d, 6-a, 7-j, 8-f, 9-h, 10-b

53.

1. They were "determined by 'Your Hit Parade' survey which checks the best-sellers in sheet music and phonograph records, the songs most heard on the air and most played in the automatic coin machines—an accurate, authentic tabulation of America's taste in popular music."
2. Raymond was your host; Bromo Seltzer sponsored it
3. "Information Please"
4. A. L. Alexander
5. "The Adventures of Nero Wolfe"
6. Jonathan Kegg was "The Friend of The Court"
7. Alexander Woollcott
8. "The Aldrich Family"; Ezra Stone played Henry Aldrich
9. "The A&P Gypsies"
10. Bill Stern, the Colgate Shave Cream Man

54.

1. The United Fruit Company
2. The Pennsylvania
3. a) soap; b) department stores; c) motion pictures
4. Durant was a bull; Livermore was a bear
5. An electrical utilities tycoon
6. a) dye in soap form; b) silk hosiery; c) toothpaste
7. The Gold Dust Twins
8. He drew the men in the Arrow collar ads
9. Force Cereal
10. Herpicide

55.

1-b, 2-e, 3-g, 4-j, 5-l, 6-o, 7-d, 8-m, 9-h, 10-a, 11-n, 12-f, 13-k, 14-i, 15-c

56.

1-e, 2-d, 3-h, 4-i, 5-f, 6-c, 7-j, 8-g, 9-a, 10-b

57.

1. Nicholas Murray Butler, president of Columbia University
2. Fala was a Scotch Terrier
3. To win a $25,000 prize
4. a
5. The giant panda
6. c
7. Automatic dialing was introduced
8. Discovery of insulin
9. "The forgotten man"
10. Huey Long

58.

1. *Little Caesar*
2. *The Werewolf of London*
3. *The Invisible Man*
4. *The Thing*
5. *King Kong*
6. *Gone With The Wind*
7. *I Am a Fugitive from a Chain Gang*
8. *The Maltese Falcon*
9. *Mandalay*
10. *Kid Galahad*

59.

1-e, 2-g, 3-i, 4-c, 5-f, 6-a, 7-h, 8-d, 9-j, 10-b

60.

1-d, 2-f, 3-i, 4-j, 5-l, 6-a, 7-o, 8-n, 9-m, 10-k, 11-e, 12-h, 13-g, 14-c, 15-b

1. *Arsenic and Old Lace*
2. *Lady in the Dark*
3. *Grand Hotel*
4. *Laura*
5. *The Paradine Case*
6. *Native Son*
7. *Watch on The Rhine*
8. *The Blue Dahlia*
9. *Three Strangers*
10. *Dark Waters*

1. Al Jolson
2. Anita Loos
3. Dorothy Parker
4. Robert Ripley
5. Mae West
6. Westbrook Pegler
7. Duke of Windsor (King Edward VIII)
8. Joe Jacobs
9. Noel Coward
10. Greta Garbo

1. Joey Adams
2. "Washington Square" and "Where's Raymond"
3. Imogene Coca, Nanette Fabray, Janet Blair, and Giselle Mackenzie
4. Eve Arden
5. Mike Barnett
6. Marvin Miller played Michael Anthony on "The Millionaire"
7. a) Broderick Crawford; b) Laurie Anders; c) Dave Garroway
8. They all played TV attorneys
9. They were all maids
10. "Pantomime Quiz"

64.

1. a) *Show Boat*; b) *The Sun Also Rises*; c) *Main Street*
2. d
3. In *Hamlet* (*Act III, Sc. 4*)
4. b
5. Owen Johnson
6. a) Pennsylvania, John O'Hara; b) New York (Long Island), F. Scott Fitzgerald; c) Mississippi, William Faulkner; e) Ohio, Sinclair Lewis
7. Arthur Kober
8. *Revelry*
9. Sauk Center, Minnesota
10. Eleanor Roosevelt's syndicated newspaper column

65.

1. Sherwin-Williams paint
2. Wrigley's gum
3. Maxwell House Coffee
4. Buick
5. Life Savers
6. Melachrino
7. Cascarettes
8. Chesterfields
9. Lucky Strikes
10. Longines

66.

1. a
2. d
3. It was the total number of electoral votes Alf Landon received
4. Prince of Wales; Duke of York
5. New Jersey

6. c
7. a) style of singing; b) fainting, usually brought
   about by (*a*); c) a hair net, worn by women
   assembly line workers
8. Chain letters
9. Handies
10. Jiminy Cricket

7.

1. Jesse Owens
2. Bobby Jones
3. They were all Joe Louis Bums of the Month
4. Red Grange
5. A pro basketball team of the mid 20s
6. Sir Thomas Lipton, owner of the *Shamrock*
7. Man o' War
8. Jim Crowley and Dan Miller, halfbacks; Elmer
   Layden, fullback; and Harry Stuhldreher,
   quarterback
9. Sonja Henie
10. Tackle, fullback, end. He was probably the
    greatest all-around player of all time

8.

1. Max Steiner
2. Ricardo Cortez
3. *The Devil and Daniel Webster*
4. a) *Fleet's*; b) *Cross*; c) *Morgan's Creek*; d)
   WAVES; e) *Angels*
5. *The Cocoanuts*; b) *Monkey Business*; c) *Night
   at The Opera*; d) *Animal Crackers*
6. Huntz Hall
7. Leon Ames
8. Edgar Buchanan
9. Charlie Chase (brothers)
10. *A Free Soul*

69.

1. Mayor Fiorello La Guardia of New York City
2. Superman was faster than a speeding bullet and more powerful than a locomotive
3. Phil Baker
4. Red Ryder
5. "The Quiz Kids"
6. Oliver Queen and Britt Reid
7. The Green Hornet (Britt Reid) was the Lone Ranger's (John Reid) grand-nephew
8. Creators of *The Green Hornet* and *The Lone Ranger*
9. Red Skelton
10. Tom Mix

70.

1. "Warsaw Concerto"
2. *Male and Female, We're Not Dressing, Our Girl Friday*
3. Adrian
4. C. S. Forester and James Agee
5. a) Amy Johnson; b) Amelia Earhart; c) Eddie Rickenbacker; d) Douglas Bader
6. Joe McDoakes's "So You Want To Be a . . ." series
7. Larry, Curly, and Moe
8. *The Ghost Breakers;* Bob Hope
9. Walter Huston
10. They all played Charlie Chan

71.

1. Baer; 2. Arnall; 3. Alben; 4. Sol; 5. Vannevar; 6. Claire; 7. Raymond; 8. Donovan; 9. Fish; 10. Glass; 11. Leon; 12. Sidney; 13. Hull; 14. Pierre; 15. Vito; 16. Canada; 17. Chester; 18. Sam; 19. Gene; 20. Claude

1. Angelus Temple, Los Angeles
2. Anya Seton
3. The Princesses Elizabeth and Margaret Rose
4. a) Madeleine Carroll; b) Joan Crawford
5. Grace Kelly
6. Gloria Swanson
7. *A Tree Grows in Brooklyn*
8. Sonja Henie and Vera Hruba Ralson
9. Gertrude Ederle, August 1926
10. Jo Stafford

1. On savings stamps
2. a) suicide pilot or suicide plane; b) hurray!; c) emperor; d) suicide; e) warrior code; f) warrior
3. Alamogordo, New Mexico and Hiroshima, Japan (The Manhattan Project was the program to develop an atomic bomb)
4. V for Victory
5. The Maginot Line
6. The first American ship to fire a shot at the Japanese at Pearl Harbor
7. Iwo Jima; Joe Rosenthal
8. Freedom of speech and expression; freedom of worship; freedom from want; freedom from fear
9. Rudolf Hess
10. Leaders of Vichy France

74.

1. *Pal Joey*
2. Carmen Miranda
3. Betty Grable
4. Virginia O'Brien
5. "Beyond the Blue Horizon"
6. Fred Allen
7. *Anchors Aweigh*
8. The Andrews Sisters
9. *The Lights of New York* (not *The Jazz Singer*)
10. *Forty-second Street*

75.

1. Marcus Garvey
2. It enforced the 18th Amendment, which prohibited liquor
3. Schechter vs. U. S., invalidated the NIRA
4. Judd Gray-Ruth Snyder murder case
5. Albert B. Fall, former Secretary of the Interior
6. They had a home; Pelican in Spanish is Alcatraz
7. b
8. Nicola Sacco and Bartolomeo Vanzetti
9. The day—St. Valentine's Day
10. America went wet; the 21st Amendment put an end to Prohibition

76.

1. traps
2. Canasta, gin rummy, and pinochle
3. Miniature golf
4. The Yo-Yo
5. clockwise
6. 4
7. The Turkey Trot
8. Her fur coat
9. James J. Walker
10. planchette

77.

1. Bengué (Ben Gay)
2. Clicquot Club
3. Sapolio
4. Fisk Tires
5. Ivory Soap
6. Prince Albert
7. Puffed Wheat and Puffed Rice
8. Lux
9. Victrola and Victor records
10. Venida hair nets

78.

1. Sir Harry Oakes
2. The electric light
3. It was a TV show (a telecast of a ball game) and there were only 4,500 receivers in existence
4. A Federal Theatre Project
5. An American school of realistic painting
6. "Buck Rogers in the 25th Century"
7. He shot and killed Bruce Wayne's parents; Bruce later became Batman
8. Sinclair Lewis
9. a) Ethel Merman; b) Betty Hutton
10. He was a salesman

79.

1. d
2. d
3. c
4. None; he was 12 years old in 1914
5. Douglas "Wrong Way" Corrigan
6. It was the suspended basket
7. They were all airplane engines
8. c
9. Yes, in 1929
10. The *Hindenburg*

80.

1. James Cruze
2. Buster Keaton
3. Mary Miles Minter
4. a) *The Black Pirate*; b) *Don Q. Son of Zorro*;
   c) *Thief of Bagdad*
5. Agnes Ayers
6. Dustin and William
7. Marion Davies
8. Pola Negri
9. Pauline Frederick
10. *Son of The Sheik*

81.

1. b
2. They were all autos
3. b
4. The running board
5. c
6. Hudson
7. Chrysler
8. Jordan
9. Cadillac
10. Standard Oil Corporation of New York

82.

1. Butch Cavendish and his Hole-in-the-Wall gang
   killed Captain Daniel Reid of the Texas Rangers
   and left his young brother to die; his younger
   brother, the only Ranger left, survived to become the Lone Ranger
2. Chester Riley
3. a) Little Orphan Annie; b) Jack Armstrong;
   c) David Harding; d) Captain Midnight
4. Mel Blanc
5. Major Edward Bowes
6. Edward Arnold on "Mr. President"

7. Jack Packard, Doc Long, and Reggie Yorke
8. "Let's Pretend"
9. b
10. Senator Claghorn, Mrs. Nussbaum, Titus Moody, Ajax Cassidy, Socrates Mulligan, and Falstaff Openshaw

83.

1-h, 2-c, 3-d, 4-j, 5-f, 6-b, 7-i, 8-a, 9-g, 10-e

84.

1. Marlene Dietrich and Clive Brook
2. Montgomery Clift and Shelley Winters
3. Barbara Stanwyck and Fred MacMurray
4. Colin Clive
5. a) Don Ameche; b) Spencer Tracy; c) James Stewart; d) Joel McCrea
6. Veronica Lake
7. Jimmy Lydon
8. Lola, Rosemary, and Priscilla Lane
9. Myrna Loy and John Boles
10. Keye Luke

85.

1. DeWitt and Lila Acheson Wallace
2. *The Dearborn Independent*
3. a) Yale; b) Stanford; c) Michigan; d) Harvard
4. *College Humor*
5. a) Philadelphia; b) New York City; c) Boston; d) Chicago

86.

1. *The Gay Divorcée*
2. *Anything Goes*
3. "Begin the Beguine"
4. Cary Grant
5. *Born to Dance*
6. Mary Martin
7. a) Red Skelton and Lucille Ball; b) Betty Hutton and Bob Hope; c) Don Ameche, Janet Blair, and Jack Oakie
8. "Don't Fence Me In"
9. Alfred Drake, Patricia Morison, Lisa Kirk, Harold Lang, and Lorenzo Fuller
10. *Adam's Rib*

87.

1. It was a translation of his first name, Fiorello
2. Sunshine, food, exercise, rest, and cleanliness
3. b
4. c
5. As an excuse for a lecture on the value of thrift
6. a
7. c
8. a) Apple; b) Walk; c) Bottom; d) Hop
9. *Arrowsmith*
10. Henry George

88.

1. Bette Davis, Spencer Tracy, and Frank Capra
2. Greer Garson
3. "The Thin Man"
4. a) Preston Sturges; b) John Huston
5. *Mr. Deeds Goes to Town*
6. a) George Sanders; b) James Arness; c) Barry Fitzgerald

7. Joe Cobb, Mary Kornman, Jean Darling, Johnny Downs, Farina, Spanky Macfarland, Jackie Condon, Jackie Cooper, Mickey Daniels, Alfalfa Switzer, Darla Hood, Buckwheat Thomas
8. a) *Ivy*; b) *Angel*; c) *Miracle*; d) *Wife*; e) *Connecticut*
9. Frank Buck
10. Emil Jannings

89.

1. a) A&P Gypsies; b) Ipana Troubadors; c) Cliquot Club Eskimos
2. a) Freddy Martin; b) Kay Kyser; c) Dick Jurgens; d) Sammy Kaye
3. a) Harriet Hilliard; b) Georgia Carroll; c) Irene Daye; d Dorothy Collins; e) Ann Richards; f) Ginnie Powell
4. They were all vocalists on "Arthur Godfrey Time"
5. "Beat the Band"

90.

1. Doc Blanchard and Glenn Davis of West Point
2. Henry Armstrong—featherweight, lightweight, and welterweight champion at the same time
3. He was Commissioner of Baseball
4. The Dempsey-Tunney fight of 1927, when Tunney retained his title, even though Dempsey knocked Tunney down for 14 seconds
5. Primo Carnera
6. Wilbur Shaw
7. Ed Dunkhorst
8. Theodore "Tiger" Flowers
9. Jim Barnes
10. The Kinseys were tennis players

91.

1. Steinway Pianos
2. Chesterfields
3. Pall Malls
4. Aunt Jemima's Pancake Flour
5. The Durant auto
6. Sweet Caporal cigarets
7. Gold Medal Flour
8. Bon Ami cleaning powder
9. Fairy Soap
10. Woodbury's Facial Soap

92.

1-h, 2-e, 3-i, 4-f, 5-g, 6-d, 7-j, 8-c, 9-a, 10-b

93.

1-g, 2-i, 3-j, 4-k, 5-l, 6-n, 7-a, 8-b, 9-c, 10-o, 11-m, 12-h, 13-d, 14-e, 15-f

94.

1. Mel Blanc
2. Robert Benchley
3. Her height; she was 6'2"
4. They've all played Ellery Queen
5. They've all played Queen Elizabeth I of England
6. a) *Cry*; b) *Afternoon*; c) *Kelly*; d) *Broadway*; e) *Mars*
7. Geraldine Farrar
8. "The Falcon"; George Sanders, and his brother, Tom Conway
9. *Grand Hotel*
10. *Destry Rides Again*

95.

		American League	National League
1.	1933	Jimmy Foxx	Chuck Klein
2.	1934	Lou Gehrig	Paul Waner
3.	1935	Buddy Myer	Arky Vaughan
4.	1936	Luke Appling	Paul Waner
5.	1937	Charlie Gehringer	Joe Medwick
6.	1938	Jimmy Foxx	Erni Lombardi
7.	1939	Joe DiMaggio	Johnny Mize
8.	1940	Joe DiMaggio	Debs Garms
9.	1941	Ted Williams	Pete Reiser
10.	1942	Ted Williams	Ernie Lombardi
11.	1943	Luke Appling	Stan Musial
12.	1944	Lou Boudreau	Dixie Walker
13.	1945	George Stirnweiss	Phil Cavarretta
14.	1946	Mickey Vernon	Stan Musial
15.	1947	Ted Williams	Harry Walker

96.

1. Dr. John Brinkley
2. They were members of the Algonquin Round Table
3. Calvin Coolidge
4. They were all baseball pitchers
5. Gar Wood
6. "Be Prepared"
7. The Ozarks
8. All travel agencies
9. *If Winter Comes*, by Arthur S. M. Hutchinson
10. The textbook teaching the theory of evolution that sparked the Scopes trial in Dayton, Tenn.

97.

1-Jones; 2-Martin; 3-Hart; 4-Huston; 5-Joyce; 6-Rankin; 7-Kelly; 8-Russell; 9-Norris; 10-Sinclair

98.

1-c, 2-i, 3-g, 4-h, 5-j, 6-1, 7-n, 8-a, 9-f, 10-m, 11-k, 12-e, 13-o, 14-d, 15-b

99.

1. b
2. a
3. a
4. a) Small towns turned thumbs down on films with rural settings; b) stock market crash; c) a Buffalo, N.Y., blizzard hurt local theater business
5. The Hall-Mills murder case
6. c
7. They were all dime novel heroes
8. They were radio sports announcers
9. Balto, the husky
10. b

100.

1. E. A. Dupont
2. Bashful, Grumpy, Sneezy, Sleepy, Happy, Dopey, and Doc
3. African wild animals
4. Harold Lloyd
5. Fred Newmer
6. Colleen Moore
7. Renee Adoree
8. The ever-popular Mae Busch
9. Bugs Bunny
10. Dagwood Bumstead's

101.

1. Forhan's Toothpaste
2. Old Dutch Cleanser

3. Palmolive Soap
4. Packard auto
5. Fatima Cigarets
6. Mellin's Foods
7. Jell-O
8. Fletcher's Castoria
9. Child's Restaurants
10. Peter's Milk Chocolate

102.

1. a) "Big Jon and Sparky"; b) "The Big Show"; c) "Big Sister"; d) "The Big Story"; e) "Big Town"
2. Don Ameche and Frances Langford; Danny Thomas
3. Mishel Piastro conducted the Longines Symphonette; Frank Knight was the announcer
4. "Screen Guild Players," "Screen Directors Playhouse," and "MGM Radio Theatre"
5. "Lucky Strike Means Fine Tobacco"
6. Paul LaValle
7. Mortimer Snerd, Effie Klinker
8. "Jack Armstrong, the All American Boy"
9. "Curtain Time" and "Knickerbocker Playhouse"
10. Amos 'n' Andy

103.

1. Lionel Barrymore
2. Olivia de Havilland
3. Walt Disney
4. They've all played Benjamin Disraeli
5. Anna May Wong
6. Shaw
7. Barbara Bel Geddes
8. Minnie Mouse
9. They both played Little Orphan Annie in the movies
10. a) Belita; b) Bourvil; c) Cantinflas; d) Capucine

104.

1. *The Best Short Stories*
2. Henry Drummond
3. *Gone With the Wind*
4. Anatole France
5. Anne Morrow Lindbergh
6. Contributors who entered jingle contests held each summer; the winners were paid $100.00 for each jingle accepted
7. William Randolph Hearst
8. They were all newspaper columnists
9. a) *The Literary Digest*; b) *Vanity Fair*; c) *Saturday Evening Post*; d) *The Atlantic Monthly*; e) *The American Mercury*
10. He contributed most of the medical background

105.

1. The Empress Carlotta, widow of Maximilian of Mexico
2. c (in 1927)
3. a) William Howard Taft; b) William D. Haywood; c) William T. Tilden II, and d) William H. Thompson
4. An illustrator and cartoonist
5. They were all members of comedy teams
6. Franklin Pierce Adams
7. Harry
8. Made the first blind flight in history
9. Henry Ford
10. Knute Rockne

106.

1-c, 2-e, 3-g, 4-i, 5-j, 6-h, 7-d, 8-f, 9-b, 10-a

107.

1. "Backstage Wife"
2. "The Bob Hawk Show"

3. The panel was Senator Ford, Harry Hershfield, and Joe Laurie, Jr.; Peter Donald was the joke teller
4. "The Chamber Music Society of Lower Basin Street"
5. He was the Crime Doctor
6. The Old Ranger
7. "Dr. I. Q."
8. Edward R. Murrow
9. "The FBI in Peace and War" was sponsored by Lava Soap
10. Brad Runyon, the Fat Man, weighed 290 pounds

108.

1. Giants; 2. Cards; 3. Tigers; 4. Yanks; 5. Yanks; 6. Yanks; 7. Yanks; 8. Reds; 9. Yanks; 10. Cards; 11. Yanks; 12. Cards; 13. Tigers; 14. Cards; 15. Yanks

109.

1. The hermit of "Hermit's Cave"
2. Roger Elliott
3. Hop Harrigan
4. "Hannibal Cobb"
5. Lulu McConnell and Harry McNaughton; Tom Howard was the quizmaster
6. Casey, Crime Photographer
7. A home sweet home of their own
8. Ronald and Benita Colman
9. She played Bessie Glass in "The House of Glass"
10. Floyd Gibbons

110.

1-c, 2-e, 3-g, 4-h, 5-i, 6-b, 7-d, 8-j, 9-f, 10-a

111.

1. To fly around the world at the equator
2. To Shoeless Joe Jackson of the Chicago White Sox, during the World Series "Black Sox" scandal of 1919
3. The dinosaur
4. King Tutankhamen
5. Ignace Paderewski
6. d
7. New York City; it is the Cathedral of St. John the Divine
8. Robert Maynard Hutchins
9. Sax Rohmer
10. Warm Springs, Ga.

112.

1. *Whiz Comics, Captain Marvel Adventures,* and *Marvel Family Comics*
2. Steamboat Willie
3. Boy newscaster on Station WHIZ
4. The Vizigraph
5. Captain Nazi, Nippo, Ibac, Dr. Smash, Mr. Mind, The Orange Octopus, Herkimer the Crocodile Man
6. Solomon—Wisdom; Hercules—Strength; Atlas—Stamina; Zeus—Power; Achilles—Courage; Mercury—Speed
7. Selena—Grace; Hippolyta—Strength; Ariadne—Skill; Zephyrus—Fleetness; Aurora—Beauty; Minerva—Wisdom
8. Beautia, Magnicus, Junior, and Georgia
9. A golden thunderbolt
10. Ibis the Invincible, Spy Smasher, Lane O'Casey, Golden Arrow

113.

1-d, 2-f, 3-h, 4-i, 5-g, 6-j, 7-c, 8-b, 9-e, 10-a

114.

1-d, 2-e, 3-i, 4-g, 5-h, 6-a, 7-b, 8-f, 9-j, 10-c

115.

1. True: you play with marbles
2. True: Chief Justice William Howard Taft swore in Herbert Hoover
3. False: he was head of Local 802, the Musicians Union
4. False: Lewis Stone
5. False: Lucille LeSueur is the real name of Joan Crawford
6. False: Duke was Tim Holt's horse, Elliott's horse was Sonny
7. False: she was a riveter
8. True
9. True
10. False: it was Dorothy Thompson

116.

1. Adolf Hitler takes over Germany; he was an Austrian
2. FDR's "fireside chats"
3. Birth of the Dionne quints
4. Bruno Hauptmann arrested for the Lindbergh kidnaping
5. Invasion of Ethiopia
6. Senate rejects the packing of the Supreme Court
7. The opening of the N. Y. World's Fair
8. Leon Trotsky is slain in Mexico
9. Start of the withholding tax
10. The Battle of the Bulge

117.

1-d, 2-f, 3-g, 4-h, 5-b, 6-c, 7-e, 8-j, 9-a, 10-i

118.

1-e, 2-h, 3-d, 4-g, 5-b, 6-i, 7-a, 8-j, 9-c, 10-f

119.

1. George Kelly; 2. Lou Gehrig; 3. Leon Goslin; 4. Lloyd James Waner; 5. Mordecai Peter Brown; 6. Charles Leo Hartnett; 7. Stanley Raymond Harris; 8. George Edward Waddell; 9. John Joseph Evers; 10. Leo Durocher

120.

1. a) Charles Curtis; b) John Nance Garner; c) Henry A. Wallace; d) Harry S Truman; e) Alben W. Barkley
2. Thomas R. Marshall; Wilson's vice president
3. They were all U.S. Attorney Generals
4. Frank Knox
5. Arthur Capper
6. Franklin Delano Roosevelt and Winston S. Churchill met to sign the Atlantic Charter
7. James, Elliott, John, and Franklin D. Roosevelt, Jr. Their mother was Eleanor Roosevelt
8. The Civil Works Administration
9. a) Secretary of State; b) Postmaster General; c) Secretary of Interior; d) Secretary of the Treasury
10. A 21-inch female midget sat on his lap

121

1. *Anna Christie*
2. Daisy
3. They were all angels
4. Amnesia
5. Monogram Pictures
6. *Algiers*
7. Rin Tin Tin
8. Hedy Lamarr
9. *Adventure*
10. Spencer Tracy (lookalikes)

122.

1-c, 2-e, 3-g, 4-i, 5-j, 6-h, 7-a, 8-d, 9-f, 10-b

123.

1. *The Big Parade*
2. Robert Taylor
3. *Adam's Rib*
4. Duke Mantee
5. Elmo Lincoln, Gene Polar, P. Dempsey Tabler, James Pierce, Frank Merrill, Johnny Weissmuller, Herman Brix, Buster Crabbe, Glenn Morris, Lex Barker, Gordon Scott, Denny Miller, Jock Mahoney, Mike Henry
6. a) Charles Laughton; b) George Sanders, Anthony Quinn; c) Jose Ferrer; d) Kirk Douglas; e) Charlton Heston
7. Robert Flaherty
8. a) Jack Haley; b) Ray Bolger; c) Bert Lahr; d) Margaret Hamilton; e) Frank Morgan
9. Vincent Price, in *The House of Wax*
10. James Arness

124.

1. a) Women's Auxiliary Army Corps (Army); b) Women Appointed for Voluntary Emergency Service (Navy); c) Women's Auxiliary Ferrying Squadron (Air Corps); e) Semper Paratus Always Ready Service (Coast Guard)
2. OPA (Office of Price Administration)
3. They were all rationed
4. Douglas MacArthur
5. It was the run on nylons before they disappeared from the market
6. Montgomery Ward's offices were taken over by the U.S. Army, following the firm's refusal to obey War Labor Board directives
7. They were indicted as seditionists in 1942 (the indictments were later dismissed)
8. b
9. She was the sole dissenting vote against a unanimous declaration of war against Japan on Dec. 8, 1941
10. The Jeep

125.

1. a) "America's Hour"; b) "America's Lost Plays"; c) "America's Town Meeting"
2. "Al Pearce and His Gang"
3. "Arthur Godfrey Time"
4. Frank Lovejoy was in "The Amazing Mr. Malone," and Keenan Wynn starred in "The Amazing Mr. Smith"
5. "The Big Story"
6. Boston Blackie
7. "Mr. and Mrs. North"
8. "Meet Me at Parky's"
9. Mandrake the Magician used to invoke the law of magic
10. The Mysterious Traveler

126.

1. A zoot suit
2. A full-dress coat
3. An admiral's dress hat
4. A tin can
5. A stiff shirt front
6. A baby's petticoat buttoning at the shoulders
7. Alice Roosevelt Longworth, Teddy Roosevelt's daughter
8. A straw hat
9. Eyeglasses kept in place by a spring pinching the nose
10. Strips of cloth wound spirally around the leg from ankle to knee

127.

1-c, 2-f, 3-d, 4-i, 5-g, 6-a, 7-h, 8-e, 9-j, 10-b

128.

1-d, 2-j, 3-h, 4-n, 5-f, 6-a, 7-e, 8-m, 9-c, 10-l, 11-b, 12-g, 13-o, 14-i, 15-k

129.

1. Haile Selassie
2. A Manhattan prison
3. Paavo Nurmi
4. Lon Chaney
5. Helen Wills Moody
6. Gilmour Dobie, of Cornell
7. David Belasco
8. John Philip Sousa
9. Babe Ruth
10. An executive serving in a government post for a token salary.

130.

1. The Ku Klux Klan
2. The Salvation Army
3. The Boy Scouts
4. a) International Order of Odd Fellows; b) Fervent Order of Eagles; c) Woodmen of the World; d) Knights of Pythias; e) Knights of Columbus; f) Benevolent and Protective Order of Elks
5. Rotary
6. The Oxford Group, also known as the Buchmanites
7. Argentina, Brazil, and Chile
8. International Workers of the World (IWW, or "I Won't Work")
9. The film industry's self-censorship agency
10. The Women's Christian Temperance Union

131.

1. They all played Santa Claus
2. Basil Rathbone
3. He let his voice assume its normal pitch (he was disguised as an old woman)
4. a) Marie McDonald; b) Lauren Bacall; c) Betty Grable
5. Gypsy Rose Lee
6. "Vampires DO exist"
7. Boris Morros
8. Chester Morris
9. *Morocco*
10. Charlie Chan

132.

1-e, 2-h, 3-d, 4-j, 5-g, 6-a, 7-b, 8-i, 9-c, 10-f

133.

1-d, 2-e, 3-p, 4-g, 5-k, 6-j, 7-l, 8-o, 9-m, 10-n, 11-h, 12-a, 13-i, 14-f, 15-b, 16-c

134.

1. Political mavericks from the Northwest
2. The First Battalion of the 308th Infantry and parts of the 306th and 307th Infantry Machine Gun Battalion of the 77th (N.Y.) Division, believed lost but later found (1918)
3. Ivar Kreuger
4. 3-day suspension of banking operations in 1933
5. President Franklin D. Roosevelt's advisers
6. Fifth Avenue buses with two stories
7. The motto on NRA stickers and signs
8. Our stated objective in Latin American affairs
9. Harold Ickes
10. A rough translation of the Japanese phrase meaning suppression of anti-government ideology

135.

1. b
2. a
3. b
4. a) drug addict; b) detective; c) uniformed policeman; d) pickpocket; e) pistol
5. The four Railway Brotherhoods
6. the printers' union
7. U. S., England, and Russia
8. Street cleaners
9. Vice President John Nance Garner
10. Vice President Alben W. Barkley

136.

1-c, 2-e, 3-h, 4-b, 5-f, 6-g, 7-a, 8-d

137.

1. Joe Corntassel
2. Lenore Case ("Casey")
3. Henry Aldrich's girlfriend
4. Lorelei Kilbourne
5. The Southern belle on "The Great Gildersleeve"
6. Detective Dan McGarry
7. Perry Mason
8. The lovely Margot Lane
9. Sherlock Holmes
10. Casey, Crime Photographer

138.

a) Diablo; b) Scout; c) Trigger; d) Tony; e) Buttermilk; f) Tarzan; g) Rex; h) Victor; i) Silver; j) Champion

139.

1. Cuba Libre
2. A Bronx
3. An aspirin in Coca-Cola
4. Moxie
5. a
6. Champagne
7. a) rye and Coca-Cola; b) Tom Collins; c) rye highball; d) whisky and soda
8. Ships smuggling liquor
9. A Prohibition agent team
10. A Methodist Church official and leader of the "drys"

140.

1. *Saboteur*
2. Butch
3. Paul Muni
4. Margo
5. Hugh Herbert
6. *Hell's Angels*
7. They're all from *Gold Diggers of 1933*
8. "Hurray for Hollywood" was sung by Dick Powell in *Hollywood Hotel*
9. Skippy Homeier
10. Dolores Del Rio and Gene Raymond

141.

1. d
2. 102 stories
3. The Woolworth Building, N. Y. C.
4. The Waldorf-Astoria
5. Rochester, N. Y.
6. Temporary shack communities built during the depression
7. Gutzon Borglum
8. Henry J. Kaiser
9. A building shaped like a flatiron in New York City
10. Frank Lloyd Wright

142.

a) cornet; b) trombone; c) alto sax; d) tenor sax; e) baritone sax; f) clarinet; g) piano; h) guitar; i) bass; j) vibes

143.

1. They were both drummers with Tommy Dorsey
2. Bon Bon
3. Bea Wain
4. RCA Victor
5. The Charleston
6. "Let's Dance"
7. "Swing into Spring"
8. Georgia Gibbs
9. Florian ZaBach
10. Helen O'Connell

144.

1-c, 2-e, 3-g, 4-j, 5-i, 6-h, 7-a, 8-d, 9-f, 10-b

145

1. FM radio
2. They all developed machine guns
3. He developed Coca-Cola
4. The rocket
5. Polaroid glass
6. Fred Waring
7. Luther Burbank
8. The automobile self starter
9. Dr. Paul Ehrlich
10. Radar

146.

1-c, 2-c, 3-a, 4-b, 5-a, 6-b, 7-b, 8-a, 9-a, 10-a, 11-a, 12-b, 13-b, 14-a, 15-a

147.

1. "Renfrew of the Mounted," "Sergeant Preston of the Yukon" ("Challenge of the Yukon"), "Silver Eagle, Mountie"
2. Her mother-in-law
3. The Sammy Kaye orchestra
4. Commissioner Westin
5. "The Romance of Helen Trent"
6. "Road of Life"
7. "Portia Faces Life"
8. A "Magic Violin"
9. "Pat Novak, For Hire"
10. The inner seal from a jar of Ovaltine, together with 10¢ to cover the cost of mailing and handling

148.

1. *The Painted Desert, Honky Tonk, Across the Wide Missouri, Lone Star, The Tall Men, The King and Four Queens, The Misfits*
2. A villain, played by Walter Houston, in *The Virginian*
3. *California, Copper Canyon, Bugles in the Afternoon, A Man Alone*
4. *The Kissing Bandit, Johnny Concho, Sergeants Three, Four for Texas*
5. *The Treasure of the Sierra Madre, A Holy Terror, The Oklahoma Kid, Virginia City*
6. George "Gabby" Hayes, Jimmy Ellison, Russell Hayden, Andy Clyde, Jimmy Roger, Jay Kirby, Brad King, and Rand Brooks
7. *The Oklahoma Kid, Run for Cover, Tribute to a Bad Man*
8. Jeff Chandler
9. Warner Baxter, Cesar Romero, Duncan Renaldo, Gilbert Roland
10. *Johnny Guitar, Winners of the Wilderness, Law of the Range, Montana Moon*

149.

1. Singing Sam, the Barbasol Man
2. "When a Girl Marries"
3. "Terry and the Pirates"
4. Ralph Edwards
5. Jack Dempsey, Clara Bow, and Jack Benny—the mystery stars on "Truth or Consequences"
6. "Take It or Leave It"
7. "They were well calculated to do so"
8. "Strike It Rich"
9. Stella Dallas
10. Joseph M. White

150.

1. Norway
2. Kaiser Wilhelm of Germany
3. Albert of Belgium
4. "Marie"; Queen Marie of Roumania
5. The King and Queen of England
6. The King of England (Emperor of India in Hindi)
7. b
8. No—George V was
9. *King Kong*
10. Wayne King